The Literature of Provence

The Literature
of Provence

An Introduction

DANIEL VITAGLIONE

McFarland & Company, Inc., Publishers
Jefferson, North Carolina, and London

Acknowledgments: I would like to thank the following people for their assistance and information: Muséon Arlaten, Marie-José Fassiotto, Jean-Claude Izzo, Marie-Thérèse Jouveau, Claude Girault, Pierre Magnan, and the following editors and associations for their photographs: Laurent Aubanel, Denoël, Gallimard, Grasset, de Fallois, Laffont, Table Ronde. L'Amitié Henri Bosco, Les Amis de Jean Giono, and the Palais du Roure. Finally, I would like to thank my wife Heather Buckner Vitaglione for her pertinent advice and computer skills.

Library of Congress Cataloguing-in-Publication Data

Vitaglione, Daniel, 1949–
    The literature of Provence: an introduction / Daniel Vitaglione
        p.   cm.
    Includes bibliographical references and index.
    ISBN 0-7864-0843-X (softcover : 55# alkaline paper) ∞
    1. French literature—France—Provence—History and criticism.   I. Title.
    PQ3803.P7V58   2000
    840.9'9449—dc21   00-61662

British Library Cataloguing data are available

On the cover: Frédéric Mistral, 1830–1914 *(photograph: Palais du Roure, Avignon)*

Manufactured in the United States of America

*McFarland & Company, Inc., Publishers
    Box 611, Jefferson, North Carolina 28640
    www.mcfarlandpub.com*

To my children,
Sylvie and Julian Vitaglione

Contents

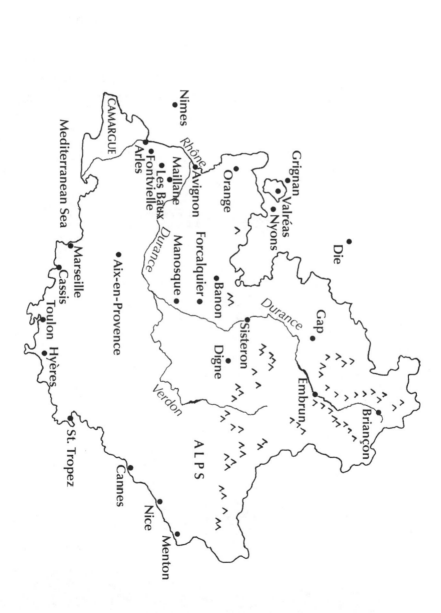

Mediterranean Sea

CAMARGUE

Nîmes

Rhône

Arles
Fontvielle
Avignon
Maillane
Les Baux

Orange

Grignan
Valréas
Nyons

Die

Durance

Marseille
Cassis
Toulon
Hyères

Aix-en-Provence

Forcalquier
Manosque

Banon

Durance

Gap

Sisteron

Digne

Embrun

Briançon

Verdon

St. Tropez

Cannes

Nice

A L P S

Menton

Preface

Provence occupies the southeastern part of France from the Rhône river in the west to Italy in the east. In the north it extends to the lower Alps. Within these natural boundaries lies a region characterized by a Mediterranean climate, mild winters and hot and dry summers. Temperatures are more continental inland, in higher Provence, and moderate on the coast. A powerful and cold wind or *mistral* blows south but affects only western Provence. The region's homogeneous nature has fashioned its inhabitants over time and given them their specific temperament. But to the natural boundaries one must add cultural and linguistic ones. Provence is the place where Provençal is spoken and French pronounced *à la Provençale*. These linguistic boundaries are more clearly marked in the north, where, past Montélimar, one begins to speak French with an *accent pointu,* according to Provençals. In the west the difference is not as marked, but around Nîmes begins the land of Occitan, a language akin to Provençal but in many ways closer to

1

Catalan. There the regional pronunciation of French changes slightly, the "r" becomes gently rolled and *année* is pronounced with a double "n." To the east, Provence stops at the Italian border but the dialects spoken there are closer to the Italian dialects spoken around San Remo.[1]

Archeology shows that humans have inhabited the area for at least one million years. Successively occupied by Ligurians, Celts and Greek settlers on the coast, in the first century B.C. this land was colonized by the Romans and became their *Provincia*. These four cultures blended into one another and gave the region its specificity and force. It subsequently resisted northern invaders, Visigoths and Franks (fifth and sixth centuries) and Arabs (eighth and ninth centuries). Between the ninth and the eleventh centuries, Provence passed into the hands of the heirs of the Carolingian Empire and finally into those of the Counts of Toulouse. From the twelfth to the thirteenth centuries it was ruled by Catalan kings who were finally forced to become allies of the French kings. In 1246, Charles d'Anjou, brother of King Louis IX of France, married Béatrice, daughter of the last Catalan king, and Provence passed into the Anjou branch of the French royal family. In 1481, the king of France definitively annexed Provence. Its eastern frontiers underwent several changes since Nice and its higher country became part of the kingdom of Savoy in 1388. Except from 1705 to 1713 and 1792 to 1814, when it was occupied by France, Nice remained in the hands of Savoy until 1860.

Despite its annexation by France, Provence has managed, even to this day, to keep its culture and language. Provençal was still widely spoken until World War II and has been taught in the schools as an elective since the 1970s. Provençals have generally accepted their attachment to France, but they have never renounced their differences and are proud of their customs and language. To them, Provence is more than a climate, a *cuisine* or an accent. It is a way of life and thinking deeply rooted in Roman culture which, over two thousand years, has perpetuated itself with a constant flow of Italian immigrants.

Provençal identity is also visible in its long literary tradition. From the troubadours to the twentieth century, Provençals have written poems, novels and plays in their language. The choice of language was a statement of cultural identity. But more recently, in order to reach a larger audience and make a living from their writing, others chose to express themselves in French; but their Provençal culture permeated their language and, as Mistral said of Daudet, they sang Provençal in French. Unfortunately, Parisian publishers in quest of clichés and local color too often misinterpret Provençal authors, and critics mostly ignore the

tradition that inspired them. The purpose of this book is to go beyond the usual clichés and common misconceptions and show the existence of a genuine indigenous tradition.

The literature of Provence was never impermeable to outside influences and, in fact, like all other literature, certainly benefited from them. Mistral appreciated Lamartine to whom he owed his fame; Daudet was forever grateful to Flaubert who also helped him become a successful writer and Gide was certainly instrumental in the publication of Giono. Giono loved Stendhal, and Magnan immersed himself in Proust for years. Such influences cannot be easily dismissed, but their role was generally limited to a few technical aspects. For their true inspiration, Provençal authors turned to their region and especially to the example of their local predecessors. Mistral considered himself a modern troubadour and his talent inspired generations of writers from Daudet to Henri Bosco, Marie Mauron and Sully André Peyre. Giono is essentially a man of the high plateaus above Manosque and his work inspired in turn Pagnol and Magnan.

Provence has two sides. At first glance, humor and affability seem to dominate and Provençals remind the Northern traveler of Tartarin or César. But a more discriminating look shows a dark side. "La Provence n'existe vraiment que dans ce qu'elle tait" (Provence truly exists by what she does not say), declares Yvan Audouard who reminds foreigners that, contrary to common belief, Provençals are above all prudent, reserved, and secretive.[2] Mistral once told the story of an old countryman who passed a rope around his neck and jumped into the Rhône. Fortunately someone who had observed the scene dove into the river and saved him. The old man was thankful, but as soon as the traveler left, he jumped back into the river. The man saved him a second time and then a third time after which he seriously scolded the old Provençal, who finally promised to go home. The perplexed traveler watched one last time the peasant with his rope walk away towards an olive grove. On the next day, the *gendarmes* arrested the traveler. The old man had in fact hanged himself to an olive tree! Asked why he had not assisted the victim, the traveler frowned and answered that when he saw the old man walk toward the trees with his rope, he thought he was going to dry himself out. Provence hides behind its affability and humor but its spirit is in truth pervaded by mystery and a keen awareness of the tragic sense of life.

This book is only an introduction aimed at the general reader and limits itself to the most famous authors, those for whom Provence played

a major role and who, to paraphrase Audouard again, always lived with it.[3] Therefore, Emile Zola, Edmond Rostand, Charles Maurras, André Suarès, Albert Cohen and many others, in whose works Provence played only a secondary role, are not included. Translations, unless otherwise indicated, are my own.

Endnotes

1. The *Rhodanien* dialect is spoken in Eastern Provence, *Gavot* inland. *Nissart,* spoken in Nice, is closer to Provençal than *Monegasque,* used in the Principality of Monaco, which is linguistically a Ligurian dialect. Poet Louis Notari (1879–1961) first codified Monegasque into a written language. Provençal, including *Nissart*, has been taught in the schools since the late 1970s. According to Philippe Blanchet, only 10 percent of the population use Provençal on a daily basis and 20 percent from time to time, but 60 percent understand it. *Dictionnaire du Français régional de Provence* (Paris: Bonneton, 1991) 147.

2. Yvan Audouard, *Ma Provence* (Paris: Plon, 1993) 11.

3. "Je ne vis pas toujours en Provence mais je vis toujours avec elle." Audouard, 7.

One

From the Troubadours to the Revolution

In medieval Provence, as throughout the southwestern region of France, Trovatores or troubadours handed down literary culture. The latter generally wrote and sang their own poems often accompanied with a viela, or hired *Joglars* to do it for them. Although they were primarily known for their *cansos* or love poems, the troubadours also wrote ballads, *dansas* or dance songs, pastourels, *tensos* with several players, *planhs* or funeral complaints, as well as moral and political satires or *sirventes*.[1] There was also a long epic tradition but unfortunately only two pieces have survived: *Jaufré* (end of 12th century) and *Flamenco* (13th century), a poem composed of 8085 octosyllabic verses, now preserved in the city library of Carcassonne. It is difficult for scholars to decipher the musical notations of the troubadours largely because of a lack of information on meter and rhythm and they unfortunately remain very

cryptic. *Cansos* show a wide array of originality as far as form is concerned, although there seems to be a common preference for a stanza divided into two parts, a *fronds* made up of two identical sections of *pedes*, and a *cauda* usually from three to six lines long.[2] The art of the troubadours was not the prerogative of one social class and historiography shows that whereas some belonged to the local nobility, others were *bourgeois* or even members of the clergy. Many traveled and sung their songs from castle to castle, but some preferred to remain within their own homes. Women or *Trobairitz* also composed and sang their poems. There does not seem to be a particular religious creed either, for some troubadours were Cathars and led ascetic lives, practicing compassion and poverty, while others remained Catholics.

The troubadours of Provence did not represent a separate caste but always remained in contact with their fellow writers in the Limousin or Gascony regions, although their language already reflected some regionalism. Biographical information on the troubadours in general is scanty and, unfortunately, very few of their works have survived, which limits our understanding of their art. Most of the *sirventes* and epics have mysteriously disappeared and only a few lyric poems have survived. For Provence alone, Alfred Jeanroy cites names of forty-eight *Trovatores* but little is known about them. Raimbaut of Orange (Rambautz d'Arenga: 1144–1173) is the most ancient. The son of Guillaume d'Omelas and Tiburge of Orange, Raimbaut resided in the castle of Courthezon and his court entertained many a famous poet. According to legends, Raimbaut "amèt longa sason une domna de Proensa, que avia nom ma domna Maria de Vertfuoil; et apellava la 'son Joglar' en sas chiansos. Longamen la amèt et ella lui." (He loved a Provençal Lady by the name of Mary of Vertfuoil whom he called his Joglar in his poems. He loved her for a long time and she him.)[3] He was also in love with Countess of Urgel whom he had never met. His two daughters Tiburge and Tiburgette inherited his estates. Thirty-nine poems have survived: mostly *cansons*, one *sirventes* and one *tenson* of which the following stanza is an excerpt:

Don', Amors a tal mestier,	Lady, Love was invented so
Pus dos amics encadena,	That when two lovers are enchained
Que' l mal qu'an e l'alegrier	Whether they feel pain or joy
Sen chascus, ço'lh ees vejaire.	Each one feels the same.
Qu'ieu pens, enon sui gabaire,	I think that, and I do not jest,
Que la dura dolor coral	For the sharp pains of the heart
Ai eu tota a mon cabal.	I bear the whole burden.

The troubadour Raimbaut of Vaqueiras (1155–1207) was the son of an impoverished Provençal knight by the name of Peirols who was said to be mad ("Filli d'un paubre chavalièr c'avia nom Peirols, qu'èra tengut per mat").[4] Raimbaut became a Joglar and resided first in Orange and then at the court of Guillaume des Baux who admired his singing. He also worked for the Marquis of Montferrat whom he followed to Constantinople in 1202. It is generally believed that he died in Salonica in 1207 fighting by the side of the Marquis, although some scholars think he came back to Provence and died there shortly after. He left thirty-three *cansos*. He was one of the first troubadours to introduce lyric poetry in Italy and had a lasting influence on Italian poets, particularly on Dante.

Domna grazida,	Sweet Lady
Quecs lauz' e crida	This praise I cry
Vostra valor Qu'es abelida	Your merit that pleases
E Qui' us oblida,	And whoever forgets you
Pauc li cal vida,	Life does not enjoy
Per qu' ie'us azor, domn'eissernida;	That is why I love you, distinguished Lady
Quar per gençor vos ai chausida	For I chose you as the noblest and the best
E per melhor, de prètz compelida.	with the perfection of your merit.

About other contemporary troubadours Rostanh Berenguier, Raimon de Tors, Paulet, Bertrand Carbonel nothing is known. However, history left us some information on Folquet of Marseilles (Folquetz de Marselha), "fillz d'un mercadier que fo de Genoa et ac nom ser Anfos" (son of a merchant from Genoa named Anfos).[5] Folquet was the son of a rich Italian merchant who settled in Marscilles and was probably born around 1150. He knew the troubadours Peire Vidal and Raimbaut of Vaqueiras, was not a very learned man, but read Latin literature (Ovidus, Tacitus, and Seneca). He lived and worked in Marseilles with his wife and two sons, but sometime around 1200, he joined the Cistercian monks of the abbey of Thoronet near Toulon. He later became the bishop of Toulouse (1205) and seems to have fought for the cause of Catholicism against the Cathars. He died in 1231. About twenty poems have survived mostly *cansos*.

Dieus, que comensamens etz de tota fazenda	God who are the beginning of all things

laus vos ren c merce	I praise you and give thanks
del amor e del be	for the love and the good
que m'avetz fach ancse;	that you have always given me:
e prec, Senher, que us prenda,	and I pray you Lord, take
grans pietatz de me	great pity on me,
que no. m truep ni.m malme	that the Devil may not find me,
ni. m'engane de re	mislead me, deceive me,
Diables ni.m surprenda.	overwhelm me.
La nuech vai e.l jorns ve	Night passes, day comes,
ab clar cel et sere	the heaven is calm and bright
e l'alba no. s rete,	the dawn does not back
ans ven bel'complia.	It rises fair and full.[6]

The most famous of the ancient *Trobairitz* of Provence is undoubtedly Comtessa de Dia about whom unfortunately almost nothing is known with certainty. The original sources mention that "Si fo moillere d'En Guillem de Peitieus, bella domna e bona." She was married (perhaps to Guillaume de Poitiers) and was beautiful and virtuous.[7] She lived in the second half of the 12th century in Die, a small town in higher Provence not far from Orange. Legend mentions that she was in love with Raimbaut of Orange for whom she wrote many poems ("enamoret se d'en Rambaut de Aurenga, e fez de lui mantas bonas cansos"). Four poems have survived, two of which are incomplete. Other famous contemporary female troubadours were Grasenda de Forcalquier who left two stanzas, and Tibors, wife of Bertrand des Baux and sister of Raimbaut d'Orange, of whose works one fragment of a poem has survived. Meg Bogin argues that women troubadours came from the upper classes and that their poetry is more concrete and their style more direct than that of their male counterparts.[8] She also gives the names of two other Provençal *Trobairitz*: Almucs de Catelnau and Iseut de Capio, near Avignon, about whom unfortunately nothing is known.

Bels amics avinens e bos	Beautiful friend, gentle and handsome,
Cora.us tenrai en mon poder	When will I possess you
E que jagues ab vos un ser	If one night I lay down next to you
E qu'ie.us des un bais amoros;	And give you a loving kiss
Sapchatz, gran talan n'auria	I shall be delighted
Qu'ie.us tengues en luos del marit,	To have you instead of a husband,
Ab so que m'aguessetz plevit	Provided you swear
De far tot so qu'ieu volria.	To obey all my commands.
	—Comtessa de Dia

Pistoleta, like Folquet his predecessor, was native of Marseilles and merchant by trade who wrote and sang many poems. Guillem Rainol, a nobleman who lived in his castle on the northern slopes of the Lubéron in Apt, was known for his biting and satirical *sirventes*. Cadenet was named after the castle and village near Aix. It is said that he was captured by the Count of Toulouse who sacked his castle and took him to his court where he later wrote many beautiful poems ("el venc bod e bels e cortes, e saup bencantar e parlar, e apres a trobar coblas e sirventes").[9] Cadenet finally returned to Provence and lived in Nice. Guy de Cavaillon was known as a brave and generous knight who wrote many a popular *tenson* and love poem. He is supposed to have been in love with Grasenda, wife of Alphonse II, Count of Provence. Albert de Sisteron was the son of a Joglar whose melodies were widely admired ("Ben fo grazitz pres oloing per los bons sons qu'el fasia").[10] He lived for some time in Orange but toward the end of his life moved back to Sisteron where he died. Raimon de Las Salas was a Marseillais merchant, who like Tomier Palazi and Ricau, reputable knights from the town of Tarascon, composed many *sirventes* and *cansons*. Blacasset, Bertran d'Alamano near Eyguières, and Bertran del Pojet from Toulon are other Provençal troubadours whose poems were well known.

According to scholar Emile Ripert: "From the thirteenth to the sixteenth century the entire South forgot about the troubadours."[11] The causes of this neglect are certainly multiple but the most important one is directly linked to the persecution of the Cathars. Not all troubadours were Cathars, but the whole Southern culture suffered from the terrible repression that took place. Since the beginning of the twelfth century a new religion and way of life had developed in the southwest near Carcassonne and in Languedoc. During the crusades many Christians had come into contact with Oriental thought and particularly with the teachings of Zoroaster. Like the Oriental prophet, Cathars believed in the original coexistence of two different entities: God and Evil. According to them, God was only good and did not create nothingness. They called themselves "Pures" (Greek *Catharsis* or purification), were vegetarians, led ascetic lives, taught and practiced compassion, nonviolence, tolerance, and sexual abstinence. The fundamental dualism of the Cathars opposed the monism of the Catholic doctrine and, in 1163, Pope Alexander III accused them of heresy. In 1209, a veritable organization or Inquisition was in place to combat the heretics and rally them to the right creed. King of France Philippe Auguste, lured by the opportunity of expanding his kingdom, joined in and waged war against the Count of

Toulouse Raymond VI. The hostilities lasted thirty-three years and ended with the defeat of the Cathars who surrendered after the long siege of Montségur in 1244.

The South had been ransacked. At least ten thousand Southerners were killed and more taken prisoners. Many had fled and sought refuge in Provence and abroad. The land and properties of heretics were confiscated and the king of France forced Raymond VII of Toulouse to make his daughter Jeanne marry his son Alphonse de Poitiers. After Raymond VII died in 1249 and his daughter in 1271, Alphonse de Poitiers remained the only heir. The southwest had lost its independence, and its culture had suffered irreparable damage. Furthermore, in 1274, King Philippe Le Hardi gave Avignon and several castles around it to the Popes. The city, which had taken the side of Cathars, had been sacked in 1226 and many of its inhabitants put to death. In 1309, Pope Clement V moved into his new residence and his successors lived there until 1403. The Treaty of Tolentino finally returned Avignon to France in 1797.

After the annexation of Provence in 1481, France began a gradual but active acculturation process. In 1539, King François I issued the Ordinance of Villers-Cotterêts that replaced Latin and all other languages and imposed French. As kings became more powerful, French supplanted all other idioms and dialects and the literary productions of Provence lived in the shadow of the court poets and playwrights. Gradually French made its entry into the Provençal nobility and, following the example of the Académie Française (1635), local academies were created in Arles (1668), Nimes (1682) and Marseilles (1726). Provençal soon lost its status as a language to become a mere *patois*. In the seventeenth and eighteenth centuries, Molière, Racine, Corneille and Marivaux eclipsed all other poets and playwrights.

Nevertheless Provençal literary production survived. Louis Bellaud de la Bellaudière (1543–1588), the son of a lawyer from Grasse, studied law in Aix and wrote several poems which were collected after his death into a book entitled *Obros et Rimos Provenssalos* (Marseilles, 1595). Pierre Paul (1554–1615), a native of Salon and a friend of Bellaud's, worked as a tax collector in Marseilles where he also published one text of poetry *Lou Repenti de la Bourbouillado*. Michel Tronc composed the sonnets *Las Hunours a la Lorgino*.[12] Aixois Claude Brueys (1571–1637) wrote comedies, such as *Lou Jardin deys Musos Provensales* (1628) like Gaspard Zerbin whose work *La perlo dey Musos* appeared posthumously in 1655. Another important writer was Jean de

Cabanes (1654–1717). Son of a noble family from Aix, Cabanes wrote poems such as *L'Histourien Sincere* and burlesque tales in the manner of Boccaccio.[13]

Theater production continued to take place in Aix and Marseilles but fashion ruled and as Robert Ambart remarks: "Under the influence of Parisian drama and the specific ideas of the time Provençal playwrights moved away from their culture to give their productions a more Parisian outlook."[14] In the plays, servants and country people only spoke Provençal. Middle and upper class characters used French, which reflected the change that was gradually taking place in Provençal society. In 1575, Jean de Notredame, brother of the famous astrologer, revived the memory of the old troubadours with his *Vie des plus Célèbres et Anciens Poètes Provençaux* (1575) which later inspired Pierre Joseph de Haitze's *Apologie des Anciens Historiens et Troubadours* (1704) and Abbé Millot's *Histoire Littéraire des Troubadours* (1774). In fact, the poetry of the troubadours had not been lost but it flourished abroad, in Germany where it was closely studied by the German Minnesingers, and in Italy where it influenced Dante and Petrarch.

Endnotes

1. "Nous avons trop longtemps vécu sur le cliché du troubadour languissant devant une dame idéale en l'honneur de laquelle il compose des poèmes enflammés. Cette image d'Epinal ne saurait nous faire oublier l'engagement de ces poètes dans les affaires de leur temps…. Qui plus est, l'on pourrait affirmer, sans peur de se tromper, qu'au XIIIe siècle la poésie politique et la satire morale ont une bien plus large audience que la chanson amoureuse." Martin Maurel, *La Vielle et l'Epée: Troubadours et Politique en Provence au XIIIe siècle* (Paris: Aubier Montaigne, 1989) 11.
2. Hendrik van der Werf, *The Chansons of the Troubadours and Trouvères* (Utrecht: Oosthoek's Uitgeversmaatschappig, 1972) 60.
3. Jean Boutière et A.H. Schutz, *Biographies des Troubadours:Textes Provençaux des XIIIe et XIVe siècles* (Paris: Nizet, 1964) 441.
4. Boutière 451.
5. Boutière 470.
6. Frederick Goldin trans. In *Lyrics of the Troubadours and Trouvères* (New York: Anchor Press, 1973) 281.
7. Boutière 445.
8. Meg Bogin, *The Women Troubadours* (London: Paddington Press, 1976).
9. Boutière 501.
10. Boutière 508.

11. Emile Ripert, *La Renaissance Provençale* (Marseilles: Laffite Reprints, 1978) 25.

12. Auguste Brun, *Poètes Provençaux du XVIe siècle* (Gap: Ohprys,1954).

13. Philippe Gardy, *Un Conteur Provençal au XVIIIe siècle: Jean de Cabanes* (Aix-en-Provence: Edisud, 1982).

14. "Sous l'influence du théâtre de la capitale et des conceptions particulières de l'époque, tout cadre original s'évanouit dans les oeuvres des écrivains régionaux dont la seule préoccupation semble être d'offrir un air parisien." Robert Ambart, *La Comédie en Provence au XVIIIe siècle* (Aix: La Pensée Universitaire, 1956) 188–89.

Two

Mistral and the Félibres

The revolutionaries of 1789 tried to eradicate all other languages besides French (such as Breton, Provençal, etc.). According to them, it was essential that their ideal be understood by people all over France and so French had to be reinforced by all means. However, their efforts met resistance and Provençal remained widely spoken even after the Empire. "As soon as one leaves Marseilles, one only hears Provençal," noted J. Chabaud in 1826.[1] The situation must not have changed much by 1834, for writer Prosper Mérimée, while traveling through Provence, complained to his friend Esprit Requien that in the countryside villagers and peasants hardly knew French: "Locals neither know nor understand French."[2] Mérimée was not the only one to experience linguistic difficulties and many travelers found themselves in similar situations especially in the country. In the large towns, however, a veritable cultural transformation was taking place. Administration and commerce had forced the educated class out of

Frédéric Mistral 1830–1914 (Photograph
Palais du Roure, Avignon).

their provincialism and French became fashionable, particularly in the elegant circles of Marseilles and Aix.

Learning French was easier now than ever before and students had several French-Provençal dictionaries at their disposal such as those of Etienne Garcin (Draguignan, 1823), J. Avril (Apt, 1838) and Simon Honorat (Digne, 1839) and even a *Grammaire Française expliquée au moyen du Provençal* written by L. Masse (Digne, 1839). On the other hand, country women continued to have little or no formal schooling and therefore they remained the guardians of Provençal language and culture at least until elementary education was made compulsory and free for both sexes in 1882. Emile Ripert notes that this situation even lasted until the Great War. Unlike their wives, male peasants and artisans had managed to learn some French during their years spent away in the national armies.

Provençal literary production continued to be eclipsed by that of Paris but with the advent of Romanticism, things began to swivel back. The vogue of the novels of Walter Scott and the poetry of Robert Burns, put the Middle Ages back on the literary scene and so revived the interest in the troubadours. In his lectures at the Sorbonne, Claude Fauriel argued that the poetry of the Provençal troubadours was not only at the origin of European literature, from Dante to the Minnesingers, but fashioned its very form and spirit for centuries.[3] Fauriel also pointed out the variety of genres of troubadour poetry, reminding the audience that it was not limited to lyric poetry but also included great epics unfortunately destroyed by the Inquisition.[4] Fauriel died in 1844 but his ideas found many listening ears, especially amongst young *Félibres* such as Frédéric Mistral and Jean-Baptiste Gaut.

In the 1840s, Provençal writers got together in the cafés of Marseilles, Aix and Avignon, exchanged their ideas and created reviews and magazines. In 1841, Joseph Désénat launched *Lou Bouï-Abaisso*, and

Pierre Bellot and Louis Méry *Lou Tambourinaire et le Menestrel* both published weekly. In 1845, Jean Reboul, Reine Garde, Alphonse Maillet, and Louis Astouin, all of whom great admirers of Lamartine, launched *L'Athénée Ouvrier* which published many poems in Provençal. In Avignon, Hyacinthe Morel (1756–1829) taught rhetoric and composed songs, epistles and tales in Provençal. In Aix, where he practiced medicine, Joseph d'Astros (1780–1863) wrote fables and tales most of which were only published posthumously in 1867. Jean Diouloufet (1771–1840) of Aiguilles, near Aix, became famous for his poem *Lei Magnans* (the silk worms) and a collection of stories entitled *Fables, Contes, Epîtres, et autres Poésies Provençales* (1829). Marseillais Victor Gélu (1806–1885) was especially noted for his popular songs (*Chansons Provençales*, 1840), but, paradoxically, was not one of the foremost defenders of Provençal and argued that, before long, the language would become totally foreign to the people. Fortunately history proved him wrong.[5] In the theater, Provençal plays were still performed with as much success as in the past. In Marseilles, Carvin had written *Meste Barna* (1809), *Jean de Cassis* (1826) and *Misé Galineto* (1830). In Toulon, Pelabon wrote *Margaou et Canoro* (1836) and in Nice, François Guisol *Lou Mariagi di Conveniensa* (1842).

Meanwhile in Avignon a young boy named Frédéric Mistral wrote poems and dreamed of a Provençal Renaissance. He was born September 8, 1830, in the small village of Maillane, between Avignon and Les Baux. "La bastidasso ounte nasquère, en fàci dis Aupiho, toucant lou Claus-Crema, se ié disié lou Mas dou Juge" (The large house where I was born, facing the Alpilles hills, next to the property of the Cremas was called the Judge's Farm), Mistral writes in his memoirs.[6] The house that his father bought after the Revolution had, indeed, formerly belonged to a judge. Mistral came from a Provençal family who, except for his great-grandfather who preferred Saint-Rémy, had resided in Maillane since the fifteenth century. Initially they were simple farmers but after years of toil they finally managed to purchase their land and built their own *mas,* or farms. Mistral's father inherited the *Mas dou Juge* and settled in Maillane, where, in 1800, he married Françoise Laville, the notary's daughter. The marriage was a happy one and Mrs. Mistral later gave birth to several children but infantile mortality was then quite high and only two survived: Marie and Louis. In 1825, Mrs. Mistral died at the age of fifty-seven after a long illness. Three years later, Mr. Mistral remarried. The new bride was twenty-five-year-old Adelaide Poullinet, daughter of the former mayor of Maillane. The Poullinets were,

according to Claude Mauron, politically more to the left than the Mistrals who, like many, condemned the violence and the chaos engendered by the Revolution of 1789.[7]

The Maillane that Mistral knew as a child was a sleepy little town of some fifteen hundred people whose lives were regimented by local customs and traditions, far away from Parisian lifestyle and fashions. Its quaint cafés and shady terraces had kept their authenticity and bustled with activity. To Alphonse Daudet, a frequent visitor, Maillane resembled "an old Italian village."[8] The place could indeed boast a rich cultural past for it was first built on the ruins of a Roman temple. During the Middle Ages, the village grew steadily to about eighty-five families. The population then fluctuated following the great epidemics such as the plague of 1721, which took the lives of one hundred and twenty persons, and cholera, which, in 1845 claimed forty-five victims. The soil was rich and planted with *seisetto* or wheat, thistles, and madder. Farmers also raised sheep. Eventually silkworms were introduced and a small manufacture of wool and silk contributed to the local economy. By the 1820s, old traditional wooden tools were already disappearing, replaced by better ones made of steel or iron.

Frédéric Mistral grew up on the *mas*, two miles outside of town. "Moun enfanço proumiero se passè dounc au mas, en coumpagno di bouié, di segaire e di pastre" (As a young child I lived on the farm with plowmen, reapers and shepherds) he wrote in his memoirs.[9] On the mas, Provençal language was used almost exclusively and many of its residents, including Mistral's own mother, had little knowledge of French. Mistral quickly managed to learn the vernacular. He was an active child, eager to discover new things and naturally never missed the opportunity to accompany his father to the market in Avignon or to the fair of Beaucaire. These outings gave him the opportunity to hear French spoken by the local nobility such as the Marquis de Barbentane.

On the farm, sheltered from all outside influence, Provençal customs and traditions prevailed year round and Mistral's family celebrated all the local festivals. On Christmas Eve for instance, they invited the laborers and shared homemade *vin cuit*. The meal usually consisted of Provençal dishes such as fried cod, celery, escargots, goat cheese, olives and, for dessert, *nougat, galette* and dried figs. Over the course of the evening Mr. Mistral, who had only read three books, the Bible, *The Imitation of Christ*, and *Don Quixote*, liked to entertain his company with stories of his youth, especially with his memorable campaigns in Napoleon's army, and at midnight, the group would walk to town and

joined the villagers in church. But the *mas* was also a place where the oral tradition of story telling was maintained and, during the long winter evenings, Mistral's mother and his aunts fascinated the young boy with their tales of the *La Bèsti de Set Tèsto, Jan Cerco-la-Pou,* and *Lou Grand Cors sènso amo.* Sometimes a local shepherd joined them and entertained them with old stories from the mountains.

But happy days on the farm soon ended and, although school was not yet mandatory, Mr. Mistral wanted his son to be educated. So, at age eight Mistral walked daily the mile and half to the two-room

Joseph Roumanille 1818–1891 (Photograph Palais du Roure, Avignon).

elementary school in Maillane where Miss Teissere and Mr. Deville taught.[10] Mistral liked to recall that at that early age he did not care much for school and that, as soon he had the opportunity, he would play truant and go fishing for tadpoles in the nearby ponds or hunt rabbits. These escapades angered Mistral's father who in 1839 decided that his son should attend Saint-Michel-de-Frigolet, a boarding school a two hours' walk from their home. The school was located in an old Augustinian monastery, which after years of neglect had been entirely restored, and later purchased by a certain Mr. Donnat, an enterprising bachelor from Cavaillon, who turned it into a school. Students were recruited locally but since farmers were poor, Donnat accepted payment in kind: flour, fruit, wine, oil and vegetables, which the school cook used to feed the staff and children. The Mistrals, however, were fortunate enough to pay cash.

Winter in the old monastery was cold and bleak, but when spring came Mistral and his schoolmates enjoyed running about in the neighboring fields and fragrant hills. They played hide and seek, hunted for

mushrooms, chased rabbits and lizards or set bird-traps. A favorite recess activity of theirs was to play gold digger in the old graveyard! Whenever there was a local festival, like that of Saint Anthime in nearby Graveson, when the population prayed for rain, the whole school would attend. Mistral seems to have kept good memories of this time and he stayed there until the age of eleven. Then the school suffered internal problems mainly due to a low enrollment and after the cook left, following a unhappy love affair with a servant, Mr. Donnat chose to close it down.

In 1841, Mistral was sent to another boarding school, this time in Avignon. In those days Avignon had a rugged look, at least according to Mistral. Its fortifications were in ruins, and traffic was dense in its muddy and narrow streets. The memory of the bloody revolutionary battles still lingered on and continued to divide republicans and partisans of the Old Regime. Mr. Millet, the school principal, a big local man with "pig eyes" and "elephant feet" in Mistral's words, was, despite his looks, a gentleman, who, being native of nearby Caderrouse, also spoke Provençal fluently. Mistral liked him for he had a sincere love for poetry. Mistral improved his mathematics and reading skills and, from 1843 to 1847, also attended classes at the *Collège Royal* in the same town. His school records show that he was a fairly good student especially in Latin and Greek. In 1846, he received seven prizes.[11] But Avignon was a city where French largely prevailed and Mistral felt estranged from his *mas*. "Vers l'age de quartoge an, aquelo languitudo de moun campèstre e de ma lengo, que m'avié jamai quita, finiguè pèr me traire dins un maucor coume jamai."[12] (Toward the age of fourteen the nostalgia of my country and my language, which had never left me, eventually depressed me as never before.)Very early during his stay he deplored the regression of Provençal to the status of *patois* and swore to do everything in his power to revive it.

In Avignon, Mistral had an encounter that awakened him from his melancholy thoughts. At the *Collège Royal* he befriended a young teacher by the name of Joseph Roumanille. Born in Saint-Rémy in 1818, Roumanille, like Mistral, first mastered Provençal before learning French. Like Mistral, he was a farmer's son and the two families knew each other, but more importantly, the two companions shared the same love of Provençal and a similar desire to take an active part in its revival. Before coming to Avignon in 1845, Roumanille had taught for two years a few miles north in Nyons, where, with the help of other Provençalists such as Camille Reybaud, Eugène Lisbonne and Barthélémy Chalvet

he also organized literary soirees. He had written several poems in Provençal and French for the local newspapers, several of which were published in *Lou Tamourinaire et le Menestrel*. Roumanille corresponded with established poets such as Jean Reboul and Adolphe Dumas, and frequented Avignon's literary circles where he met writers Esprit Requien, Jean-Baptiste Gaut, Antoine Crousillat, and Castil-Blaze. Unlike Mistral, however, Roumanille was a royalist, but politics never managed to come between them.

In Roumanille, Mistral found a kindred soul with whom he could share his frustrations with the educational system and dream of a veritable Provençal renaissance. Roumanille himself had set the pace and Mistral read his poems with great admiration: "E Roumaniho, beù proumié, dins lou parla poupulàri di Provençau de vuei, cantavo dignamen, souto uno formo simplo e fresco, touti li sentimen dou cor." (Roumanille first sang in the popular language of the Provençals of his day, proudly, and in a simple and new style, all the sentiments of the heart.)[13] Roumanille, in turn, was happy to find in Mistral a student who espoused his own ideal and he introduced him to his circle of friends. The group planned a *respelido* or cultural renaissance of Provence which would restore to their language the dignity and status it was losing. Provençal, they argued, was a language and not merely a *patois* or a bastardized version of French and they set themselves the task of retrieving its pure, pristine form. Classmate Anselme Mathieu, a native of Châteauneuf-du-Pape who had a long-time interest in poetry and local folklore, joined them.

But school days soon came to an end, and in 1847 Mistral graduated. Having successfully passed his *baccalauréat*, he happily moved back home. There, in close contact with the earth, congratulated by his parents and friends, he felt like himself again. At last he was able to converse without shame in his native language. But Mistral had not lost sight of his renaissance ideal and began to collect local tales and legends, and spent many an evening listening to shepherds' stories. He had followed the political events and acclaimed the Revolution of February 1848, which forced King Louis Philippe to abdicate and leave for England. A new republic was born and all men above twenty-one years of age were granted the right to vote.

However, within the next two months, disagreements in the party and the suppression of the workers' national workshops further antagonized the bourgeois leaders from the people. On June 22, in Marseilles, barricades were erected and a battle broke out between the National

Guards and the revolutionaries who finally capitulated. Approximately twenty people were killed. The following days the streets of Paris were blocked by over four hundred barricades. The army, headed by Cavaignac, launched a bloody battle that lasted three days (June 24–26) and claimed a total of one thousand lives. Fifteen thousand Parisians were arrested a third of them deported to Algeria. Mistral was horrified and disillusioned. In December, Louis Napoléon Bonaparte, nephew of the former Emperor, was elected President of the Second Republic.

Early in the autumn, Mistral went to Aix-en-Provence and registered as a student in the Faculty of Law. This decision may seem somewhat unexpected for someone who had literary aspirations and who had never shown any particular predisposition for such a subject, but Mistral agreed with his father that for the future manager of the family farm, a law degree would prove very useful. Nestled at the foot of Mont-Sainte-Victoire, dear to Paul Cézanne, this ancient Roman spa and later capital of Provence and seat of Parliament had little in common with Avignon. More aristocratic and bourgeois, Aix was mainly the city of magistrates and professors, which gave it a more solemn atmosphere. Incidentally, eight-year-old Emile Zola, whose family had recently moved from Paris, was a student at the *Pension* Notre-Dame while Paul Cézanne, one year older, attended school Rue des Epineaux. The two boys, who later became inseparable friends, had not met yet.

Mistral lodged in town, Rue Jaubert, near the *Palais de Justice* and for the next three years attended lectures in law, studied in the library and successfully passed his examinations. But Mistral was not always reading his books and he enjoyed Aix's social life, frequented the *Cours Mirabeau* and its numerous cafés, strolled through the country to nearby Tholonet or Vauvenargues and hiked up the Sainte-Victoire. He also went to Toulon by stagecoach and on several occasions he and his friends walked to Marseilles, some eighteen miles away, where he visited the beautiful coves or *calanques,* its celebrated island or *Château d'If* and spent many a night carousing in the cafés. The student was slowly turning into a man and the years spent in Aix were also marked by romantic adventures.

The study of law did not conflict with Mistral's interest in literature and he always found time to attend poetry readings, and especially Louis Méry's seminar on Dante in the newly created Faculty of Arts. One would often see him in the old *Méjanes* library, reading Walter Scott, George Sand, Victor Hugo, Théophile Gautier, or Lamartine, but also the old troubadours. Life in Aix was exciting but Mistral had not

forgotten his old friends and regularly informed Roumanille of his activities. In 1849, Mathieu came to Aix to study law and Mistral was proud to show him around. Mistral did not miss his family as much as he had in Avignon, but was always happy to return home for the holidays.

In 1851, his last exam passed and his diploma in hand, Mistral proudly headed home again. The political situation of the country had now changed. By the coup d'état of December 1852, Louis Napoleon Bonaparte, following the example of his uncle, had declared himself Emperor. Mistral, a moderate republican, was outraged at the news and began to worry

Lazarine Nègre 1848–1899 (Photograph Alpes de Lumière, Mane).

about the future of France and of Provence. A new Empire could only mean more centralized power and less independence for the provinces and no chance for a true Provençal renaissance to take place. But Mistral never lost hope. In the meantime, he had to think about his career and his duties of manager of the family estate and he immediately set to the task. His father was now weak and almost blind and could no longer assume his responsibilities.

Work was demanding but did not conflict with Mistral's interest in local folklore. On the contrary, by its very nature it put him into close contact with the reality he wanted to study in more detail. He met with Roumanille regularly and together they took an active part in the debate on the writing and spelling of Provençal, which had never been codified. Opinions varied widely among participants and agreements were seldom reached for each preferred the particularities of their own dialect. The purists or traditionalists were partisans of a system based on etymology and of the writing used by the troubadours, others championed

the cause of phonetic writing without reference to the past. Mistral, himself, looked to Italy and Spain for examples and advocated a spelling system that would be understood by all Provencals regardless of their variety of dialect. To many, the problem seemed unsolvable.

However, things began to move. On August 29, 1852, Arles became the seat of a large meeting of Provençalists. The participants included, among others, Théodore Aubanel, Paul Giéra, Gélu, Gaut, Garcin, and Désénat. The following summer the group met again, this time in Aix-en-Provence and counted women amongst its ranks, the poets Reine Garde, Hortense Rolland, and Lazarine Nègre. The question of the spelling continued to occupy a central place but no solution was in sight. However, Gaut announced the publication of a new journal *Lou Gay Saber* (December 1853–June 1855) founded to unite all writers of langue *d'Oc*.

A larger step was taken two years later on a beautiful spring Sunday of 1854. That day, May 21, Mistral and a group of Avignon poets gathered in the castle of Font-Ségugne, near Châteauneuf-de-Gadagne, a couple of miles outside of Avignon, on the road to Apt. Exactly how many participants were there is not known but the group was small, and probably composed of seven members. Mistral's own account of the first meeting varies. In a letter to Mathieu, he mentions the names of Giéra, the host, a notary public by trade who also wrote poetry, Roumanille, Aubanel, Alphonse Tavan, A. Dau, and Ponge.[14] However in *Memori e Raconte* and the *Armana* he lists neither Ponge nor Dau but, on the other hand, mentions Jean-Gabriel Brunet of Avignon, Glaup, and Mathieu.[15] The group decided to abandon the traditional term *Troubaires* used to describe their literary activities and to replace it by that of *Félibres,* coined by Mistral.

The origin of the noun is obscure. Mistral says that he had read it in a prayer to the Virgin Mary which spoke of "the seven *Félibres* of the law," and in a letter to Gaut he further explained that a *Félibre* designated someone who wrote books ("fait libres") and that it was Roumanille who found the term in a medieval manuscript.[16] As René Jouveau suggests, perhaps the term simply sounded beautiful which, in itself, was a good enough reason to adopt it.[17] It is interesting to point out that, in order to become a *Félibre*, knowledge of the language was not sufficient and that the participants must also exert a profession which meant that their "renaissance" was also an active social movement.

Aubanel's idea that the *Félibres* should have their own review was favorably received and soon *L'Armana Provençau* (Provençal Almanach)

was born. Edited by Aubanel and supervised by Mistral, it was only published once a year but quickly became a success and, during the next three years, sold over two thousand copies. Mistral himself contributed several articles and poems such as "Lou Prégo-Dieu" (The Praying Mantis) "Une Arlatenco" (A Woman from Arles). The review rallied to its cause writers from all over Provence such as Jean Reboul (1796–1864) Adolphe Dumas (1806–1861) and Amédée Pichot (1795–1877).

Aubanel himself was a year older than Mistral. He was born in Avignon to a family of successful printers and editors. The shop had been created by his grandfather

Théodore Aubanel 1829–1886 (Photograph Editions Aubanel, Avignon).

Antoine who in 1744 left his home in Aspres-sur-Buech in the Alps and settled in Avignon. He published the *Courrier d'Avignon* and was the Pope's printer. In 1808, his son Laurent took over and improved the quality of the press to such an extent that Balzac himself asked him to print his novels. Théodore Aubanel grew up in the Rue Saint-Marc. He was a sweet, lovable child who liked to daydream. At home he spoke French but learned Provençal with his grandparents and aunts who lived outside of town in Pontet and Monteux. Later his father sent him to Aix to further his studies and when he returned home he worked in the family business with his brother Charles. Aubanel met Roumanille at the club meetings of *La Société de la Foi* and was also often a guest of the Giéras' Rue de la Banasterie or in their castle of Font-Ségune, where, in 1850, he fell in love with beautiful Jenny Manivet also courted by Roumanille and who inspired his masterpiece *La Miougrano entre-duberto* (The Opened Pomegranate, 1860). Unfortunately for Aubanel, Jenny suddenly felt a religious calling and in 1854 she joined a convent.

In 1861, Aubanel married Joséphine Mazen who gave him a son, Jean, in 1868. Aubanel's *Miougrano* attracted the attention of the public but soon became the object of severe criticism on the part of his local contemporaries and especially the religious editor of the *Revue des Bibliothèques* who found his poems too sensual and the situation lasted until Aubanel's death in 1886. The same review criticized Mistral and the *Félibres* for caring too much about poetry and not enough about Catholic morals. Nevertheless Aubanel was one of the founders of *Félibrige* and remained a good friend of Mistral and Daudet's. He also wrote for the theater (*Lou Raubatori, Lou Pastre*) but *Lou Pan Dou Pecat* is the only tragedy that was performed duriging his lifetime. His poems were later collected into books (*Li Fiho d'Avignoun, Lou Reire Soulèu*). Unlike Roumanille who believed that they should only write in Provençal, Aubanel followed Mistral in his idea of adding a French translation to his works. At all times he kept close ties with France and was opposed to the idea of separatism. On the other hand, Roumanille, who became an editor in 1855 and therefore competed with Aubanel, argued that art must serve as cause and remain essentially moral. Aubanel disagreed and, as a good republican, believed that freedom was the essential condition for creativity and that art had nothing to do with morals.[18]

In the meantime Mistral was finishing a long epic poem called *Mireio,* started around 1852. It was written in Provençal, but in order to reach a larger audience, Mistral had added a page-by-page translation in French. In 1858, he left for Paris with his Marseillais friend Ludovic Legré to attempt to find a famous author who would enjoy his poem and recommend it to a publisher. Mistral first thought of George Sand, who in the early 1840s had taken up the cause of regional literature and dialects, turning to the folklore of her native Berry for inspiration. Her tales *François le Champi,* and *La Petite Fadette* had achieved an immense success. Furthermore, Sand had encouraged Provençal poets Charles Poncy and Agricol Perdiguier and helped them publish their works. Unfortunately she was not in Paris when Mistral arrived but at her country home of Nohant some one hundred miles south where she usually spent the summer months, and Mistral had to think of someone else. Some time later however, after the publication of *Mireio,* Mistral sent Sand a copy. On March 9, 1859 she wrote him back to tell him that she had found *Mireio* beautiful, full of charm and orginality, and that she considered him one of France's finest poets.[19]

Then Mistral, advised by his friends Legré and Adolphe Dumas,

thought of Lamartine and paid him a visit. The poet asked Mistral to read aloud some passages of *Mireio* but believed it needed more work. Mistral was thankful and went back to Maillane to improve his poem. In a few months' time *Mireio* was ready and in February 1859 the presses of François Seguin in Avignon printed over one thousand copies. The book was well received by critics. Charles Rostaing counted only three negative reviews in the press.[20] Lamartine's praise was by far the most impressive. Comparing Mistral, in turn, to Homer or Burns he devoted some 80 pages of his *Cours Familier de Littérature* to *Mireio*. Mistral remained forever thankful and dedicated the second edition of *Mireio* to Lamartine.

Rose Anaïs Roumanille 1840–1920 (Museon Arlaten, Arles, photograph Delgado).

Strangely enough, except for a few reviews, the Provençal press almost ignored Mistral's poem.

Mireio is composed of twelve cantos of seven line stanzas (usually aabaaab or aabcccb, with decasyllables). In his epic poem Mistral, who describes himself as the "umble escoulan dou grand Oumèro" (humble student of the great Homer), sings the love story betwen Vincent and Mireio, "uno chats de Provenço" (a girl of Provence). The first canto begins when Mr. Ambroise, a basket maker by trade, and his son Vincent stop at the *Mas di Falabrego* owned by Master Ramon, father of Mireio. The following day Vincent and Mireio meet again in a field where she is busy working on a mulberry tree. Together they try to rescue a bird in a nest but Mireio slips off the branch and falls into Vincent's arms. The idyll is born and Mireio swears to love him forever. However, Mireio is beautiful and has many other suitors including Alàri, the rich shepherd, Véran the horse breeder and Ourrias the strong bull

herder. But her heart belongs to Vincent and she refuses to listen to her father who prefers one of the other rich herders. Alàri and Véran retreat peacefully but Ourrias is enraged and challenges Vincent to a fight. Vincent has no choice but to accept the duel. The two opponents fight bravely but as Vincent gets the upper hand he becomes less wary and Ourrias stabs him with his spear. Fearing the justice of men, Ourrias flees hurridly down the Rhône but his boat sinks and he drowns.

In the meantime, cattlemen find Vincent and take him first to Mireio's house and then to Taven, the sorceress of Les Baux, who cures him. However, Mireio's father has not changed his mind and continues to refuse Vincent as his son-in-law. Mireio decides then to go on a pilgrimage to nearby Saintes-Maries to implore God to make her father consent. But the voyage is perilous and the dangers that await her are many. She almost dies of thirst crossing the desert of Crau, suffers a severe sunstroke in the mosquito-infested marshes of Vaccarès, and when she finally reaches Saintes-Maries, she collapses and dies in the arms of Vincent, who had come, too late, to her rescue.

Mireio is above all a love story but also a hymn to the glory of Provence in all its aspects from the simple beauty of the olive fields, to its ancient Roman traditions and language. It not only brought Mistral fame but also aroused the public's interest to the social ideal of the *Félibres,* and soon writers such as Charles de Ribbe and Leon Berluc Perussis rallied to the cause. William Bonaparte-Wyse, a forty-five-year-old Irish man, was enthralled. He went to Avignon, met Mistral, and a long friendship was born. Wyse had ties with France since his maternal grandfather was Lucien Bonaparte, the Emperor's brother, but at this time he was fascinated by Mistral's ideal and decided to espouse their cause. Wyse learned Provençal and became a *Félibre.*

L'Armana Provençau found a large audience abroad and particularly among the Catalans who translated *Mireio* into their language in 1861. Encouraged by their success, the *Félibres* became more active and participated in every cultural and religious festival of Provence in Apt, Les Baux, and Sainte-Baume where the Bishop Mazenod explained that he longed to see the day when he could once again give Mass in Provençal. In 1860,with the Treaty of Turin, Nice, that had been a possession of the kingdom of Savoy-Piedmont for five centuries, returned to France and the *Félibres* were especially overjoyed to retrieve that part of Provence.

In its initial phase, *Félibrige* was a cultural and literary movement. It was peaceful and fraternal and had chosen the sun for its emblem.

But it was also well organized and at its head sat a *capoulié* or chief (Mistral) who worked in cooperation with a committee of seven elected members. Aubanel was the treasurer. Each of these members supervised in turn a group of seven *Félibres*. Each had a specific assignment. For instance Amédée Pichot and his team worked on the history, linguistics and archeology of Provence, while another section researched the arts. Section VI studied the sciences. Like the troubadours, the *Félibres* accepted women in their ranks and the list provided by Mistral in 1862 mentions the names of Rose-Anaïs Gras of Mallemort, who later became Roumanille's wife, and Countess Clémence de Corneillan of Lourmarin who chaired the science section![21] The same list also shows that the newly elected *Félibres* no longer simply came from Avignon and its immediate vicinity but also from Aix, Marseilles, Toulon, Montpellier and Nîmes. The *Félibres* renewed with the traditions of medieval *Jeux Floraux* or yearly floral festivals during which prizes were awarded to the best competitors.

But while the *Félibres* won public recognition in France and abroad, Mistral had to deal with some family problems. Following his father's death in 1855, a complex inheritance situation ensued. Mr. Mistral had been married twice and the children of his first marriage claimed their right to his estate. Louis received the *mas dou juge* where Mistral and his mother lived. Mistral inherited plots of land with farms and a house in town where he and his mother moved. It was a two-story house with a garden located on the road to Saint-Rémy and baptized *la maison au lézard*. There Mistral set to work on two fronts. First, he began another epic poem called *Calendau* and then, he formed a long-term project, the compilation of a Provençal dictionary, a comprehensive work which would rehabilitate his "venerable language." When not at work on either projects he toured the south from Béziers to Toulon giving lectures, always accompanied by his friends Roumanille and Aubanel.

Mistral was now famous. *Mireio* was reedited in 1860 and 1861. The French Academy awarded it the Monthyon prize, which was quite unexpected for a Provençal work. Two years later Mistral was made *Chevalier* and received the Legion of Honor. The theater took an interest in him and Charles Gounod, who had successfully adapted Faust for the stage, now worked on *Mireio.* The play premiered in Paris on March 19, 1864 but unfortunately failed. According to critics, Gounod had taken too many liberties with the original subject, and the public was disappointed. On the other hand, *Félibrige* or the cause of the Provençal

poets, aroused more and more interest throughout the world. In 1865, Professor Estland, from Finland, came to Provence followed by Russian Count Nicholai Semenov who settled near Avignon. Poet Stéphane Mallarmé, who then taught English in Avignon, befriended Mistral and the *Félibres*.

In May 1867, the first English translation of *Mireio* was published and Bonaparte Wyse gave a party in the castle of Font-Ségugne. Twenty-seven distinguished guests from all over Provence and Catalonia attended the celebration. For the occasion, the main dining room was decorated with medallions of the names of all the Provençal troubadours and poets. The menu consisted of an assortment of regional produce and dishes: ham from Ceyreste, olives from Aix, capers from Cuges, prawns from Aigues Mortes, *saucissons* from Arles, *pâtés* from Avignon, fresh trout from the Vaucluse, *bourride, bouillabaisse*, and for dessert *calissons* and strawberries. They drank the local Châteauneuf-du-Pape. The feast lasted three days and included a pilgrimage to the nearby Fountain of Vaucluse, in the memory of Petrarch. To thank their host, the Catalans offered the *Félibres* a silver cup or *Coupo Santo* which quickly became their "grail."

With the publication of Mistral's poem *La Coumtesso* (1866) his reputation as well as that of his poet friends began to take a different turn. The seventeen-stanza poem was a hymn to the glory of Provence before its attachment to France and sought to encourage a cultural revival. Balaguer was host of the *Félibres* and *L'Armana* now reached twenty thousand readers.[22] But in Germany, Bismark was preparing for war and many in France thought that the time was not appropriate for a regional division. What was needed was a strong France ready to face a possible German invasion. Provençals such as Charles Dupuy of Nyons, and the Marseillais Bouillon-Landais denounced the *Félibres*' ideal as obsolete and dangerous. In his book, *Des Troubadours aux Félibres,* the Marquis de Laincel argues that *Félibrige* was narrow minded and opposed to progress and Eugène Garcin, in his *Français du Nord et du Midi,* blantantly accused Mistral of separatism.

Meanwhile, *Calendau* appeared. The poem, published by Roumanille in Avignon in the winter 1867, was accompanied by a French translation, like *Mireio*. It is a love poem which takes place in the eighteenth century and tells the story of the love between Calendau and Esterello. Lady Esterello, of Les Baux, is unhappily married to Count Severan. One day she learns from her father-in-law that her husband is indeed a rogue. Shocked by the news Esterello leaves Les Baux and

wanders through Provence. In the small coastal village of Cassis she meets Calendau, a young fisherman who immediately succumbs to her charm. Esterello tells Calendau that she cannot return his love because she is already married, and explains her misfortune and her decision to leave. Her tragic situation moves Calendau and he promises to help her. In the meantime, he attempts to win her confidence and love by performing Herculean stunts such as the cutting down of the trees of Mont Ventoux and the arrest of the famous bandit Marco-mau. Still Esterello refuses to accept Calendau's advances until she is actually free to love him. Then Calendau pays Count Severan a visit in his castle of Aiglun, near Nice, and challenges him to a duel but before he can prove his strength Severan has him arrested and thrown into the dungeon. Fortunately, Calendau has more than one trick up his sleeve and manages to escape. He then seeks out Severan, finds him, and challenges him once again. After a long and difficult duel Calendau is victorious and Severan is killed. Esterello is now free to accept Calendau's marriage proposal.

Calendau was Mistral's opportunity to renew contact with the tradition of courtly love of the troubadours and to present Provençal as a "lengo d'amour." Behind the love story, however, hides ideas of "patrio"and "liberta" and Calendau is ready to fight for the cause of Provence with red canon balls if necessary. "T'apararen à boulet rouge," he proudly declares.[23] But in this poem Mistral leaves his native village for the first time to present another part of Provence, namely the world of dedicated and hardworking fishermen. The coast and its people are an important part of Provence and *Calendau* pays homage to the proud fishermen and their wives who patiently await and pray for their safe return, spin, mend clothes, and prepare *bouillabaisso*. Unfortunately, *Calendau* did not receive the same enthusiastic praise as *Mireio* and the reason lies in the political implications of the cause. Zola, a fierce opponent of the *Félibres*, reproached *Calendau* for its lack of unity. Mistral was disappointed but not discouraged.

In the spring of 1868, Mistral, Wyse, Paul Meyer and Louis Roumieux traveled to Catalonia to attend the Jeux Floraux and visited the monastery of Montserrat. The following fall, Mistral organized in his turn a festival for his Catalan friends. His presence was often solicited in cultural events and he was always willing to give a conference. Nonetheless, he still managed to find the time to write. In 1868, the *Revue des Deux Mondes* published his *Tambour d'Arcole,* and *Soulomi*, a long poem written after the death of Lamartine, appeared in

Le Journal des Débats. The war with Prussia and the defeat of France, followed by the tragic Commune rebellion in Paris in the spring of 1871, left Mistral bitter and disappointed with politics. He now slowly began to turn inwards, read Nostradamus and looked to religion for solace and inspiration. He participated in cultural events, attended the anniversary of Petrarch's death in Avignon in 1874, and welcomed the newly created *Société des Langues Romanes* in Montpellier. The rest of his time he devoted almost entirely to his dictionary.

Mistral was slowly getting on in years and he found himself thinking of marriage. He was now forty-five and decided he should find a wife so he built another house on the property. Until then Mistral had led the life of a happy bachelor and had had several relationships with women including Jeanne de Tourbey, Valentine Rostand from Burgundy, and Marie-Rose Pascalon, but none corresponded to his ideal. Eager as he was to have a family of his own, Mistral contemplated marrying Jenny Bernard, a distant cousin of his, but the bride-to-be was decidedly too homely and he quickly gave up his idea. Finally in 1876, nineteen-year-old Marie Rivière, daughter of a Burgundy friend of his, whom he had been seeing for some time, accepted his proposal and the two were married. Roumanille was his best man but Daudet, ill, was unable to attend the ceremony.

In 1876, Roumanille published Mistral's *Lis Isclo d'Or*, a collection of 91 poems, some of them composed as early as 1848, which included —in Mistral's spelling—*cansouns, sirventes, plang, sounet,* and *pantai* (dreams).

Lis enfant d'Ourfièu (cansoun)	Orpheus' Children
Sian li felen de la Greso immortalo	We are the descendants of immortal Greece
Sian tis enfant Ourfièu, ome divin!	We are your children, Orpheus, divine man
Car sian ti fieu, o Provenço countalo	Because we are your sons, O Provence of Avigno
E nosto capitalo	And our capital
Es Marsiho, qu'en mar vei jouga li doufin.	Is Marseilles which watches dolphins play in the sea.
Li Bon Provençau	The Good Provençals
D'engaugna Paris en tout	To imitate Paris for everything
Cadun s'acoumodo	Everyone attempts
E lou mounde ven pertout	And everywhere people become
Esclau de la modo:	Slaves of the fashion:

Nàutri,li bon Provençau,	We, the good Provençals
Chivalie dou Sant Grassau,	Knights of the Grail,
Faguen-nous félibre	Let us become félibres
E restaren libre.	And we will remain free.

The *Félibres* reorganized their group. Membership was now reserved to those who wrote in Provençal. The *capoulié* adopted the seven-pointed star as an emblem and along with a board of directors they made up a *consistoire*. In 1881, the first volume of Mistral's *Trésor dou Félibrige* was published in Aix-en-Provence. In 1883, Mistral's beloved mother died in Maillane at the age of eighty. The following year he published *Nerto* and attended the yearly floral games in Sceaux near Paris and was awarded the Vitet prize. The first edition of two thousand copies sold out in two weeks. *Nerto* is made up of five cantos and tells of the tragic adventure of Nerto the young and beautiful blond daughter of Baron Pons from the village of Châteaurenard, near Avignon. It is set at the end of the fourteenth century. Pope Benoît XIII is in his palace in Avignon but his reign is contested by partisans of the Roman Pope and his days are numbered. Pons is a powerful lord who spends his time waging war and gambling. One day, after having gambled and lost his fortune and castle, Pons meets the devil who offers him gold in exchange for his daughter's hand when she turns thirteen. Pons shamelessly accepts the pact and resumes his lifestyle. Years later, a few days before Nerto's thirteenth birthday he informs her of his deal and tells her to go seek the Pope's help. Nerto goes to Avignon through a secret passage but the papal palace is besieged by the partisans of the Roman Pope and she offers Benoît XIII refuge in her father's castle. The Pope accepts and after listening to Nerto's story advises her to become a nun. Nerto obeys and leaves her father. Rodrigue de Lune who is in love with her, attempts to save her but in vain. The devil reappears to confront him but before Rodrigue can fight, a thunderbolt strikes and all die.

In 1885, Mistral launched another review, *La Revue Félibréenne,* which lasted until 1909. His candidature was also solicited by various academies but Mistral, like Daudet, preferred to remain independent. *Félibrige,* he wrote to Legré, was born under the trees and the atmosphere of clubs and scholars was ill suited for it.[24] However at the death of member Aubanel in 1886, Mistral finally accepted and joined the Academy of Marseilles in 1887. In 1890, his tragedy *La Rèino Jano,* begun in 1869, was finally completed and published. In beautiful verse

it told the story of Jeanne of Anjou, Queen of Naples and Countess of
Provence (1326–1382). Wrongly suspected of having murdered her husband Andrew of Hungary, Jeanne unfortunately joined in matrimony the
veritable instigator of the murder, Louis of Tarente. Unhappy in love
she later married Jaime III of Aragon and finally Othon of Brunswick
a debauchee and a pervert. Jeanne fought her cousin Charles de Duras
and the Pope Urban VI to keep her throne but was finally defeated,
thrown in jail and smothered to death under her mattress! Mistral's
tragedy is limited to the episode of Andrew's murder and Jeanne's subsequent journey to Provence to defend herself in front of the Pope
against those who accused her of fomenting the assassination. Mistral
shows the deep affinities between the Provençals and their Queen. In
the following passage Troubadour Aufan de Sisteron boasts the merits
of his native land in the hope of enticing the Queen to journey there:

A Marsiho:la mar es vostro, lou soulèu	In Marseilles the sea is yours, the sun
E la mar soun partido atenènto à l'emperi	And the sea belong to Provence
Di Prouvençau…Venès! Veires un pople lèri	Come and you will see a joyous people
Qu'en farandoulejant vous rendra si respèt	That will dance their respect for you
E poutounejara l'estrai de vosti pèd.	And will kiss the print of your feet.
Emai un sort crudèu ague vincu Tououso	Despite the cruel destiny of Toulouse
E tra sus lou Miejour sa capo nivoulouso,	Which spread its cape of clouds over the South
Vers lou Rose i'a 'ncaro un tros de paradis	There is by the Rhône a corner of paradise
Que son flaire agradiéu à bèn luen s'espandis.	Whose beautiful aroma expands far and wide.

   In 1890, Mistral was awarded the Jean Reynaud prize for his dictionary and invested the tidy sum of ten thousand francs in a new review,
this time in Provençal, *L'Aïoli*. It was edited by Mistral, Paul Marieton,
Marius André and Folco de Baroncelli, and came out three times a month
on the presses of Seguin in Avignon. In 1888, Roumanille replaced
Mistral in the function of *capoulié,* and was himself later succeeded
by Félix Gras (1891–1901), Pierre Devoluy (1901–1909) and Valère
Bernard (1909–1914). When he was not writing or editing, Mistral traveled. He was in Paris in 1887 and 1889, in Switzerland in 1885 and in

1891 he and his wife stayed in Italy for two months. It was there, in Venice that he learned of the death of Roumanille and of Gaut, two months later. Slowly his friends were passing away. Wyse died in 1892 in Cannes.

Mistral went back to work and for months sailed up and down the Rhône taking notes, listening and talking to boatmen and old fishermen. He was, in fact, writing another epic devoted to the Rhône, simply entitled *Lou Pouèmo dou Rose* (1897) and composed of twelve cantos. Mistral's poem is melancholy throughout and evokes "the good old days" when life was slow and peaceful and people left their houses unlocked:

> "O tèms di vièi, d'antico bounoumio
> Que lis oustau avien ges de sarraio"[25]

He remembers his happy and simple childhood days when the mighty river lined with medieval castles, was still king:

> "tèms gai, tèms de simplesso
> Qu'èro lou rose un revolun de vido"[26]

and when the towns of Condrieu, Vienne or Beaucaire flourished. The poem pays homage to the Rhône's days of glory when ships like that of Captain Apian, a proud and handsome man with long curly hair and golden earrings, transported silk, leather or hemp down the river to the markets of Beaucaire, Avignon or Arles. Deep at the bottom of the river lived the evil Dra, "superbe, anguiela coume un lampre," a giant lamprey-lizard with long green hair and webbed feet and two small fins in the middle of its back who seduced and trapped many a beautiful *lanvandiero* or washerwoman. It is during a voyage on the Rhône that pretty Anglore fell in love with Prince Guilhem. But the river is deep and dangerous and their ship, caught in the middle of a violent storm, crashed and sank, and the lovers drowned. According to Mauron, the nostalgic tone of Mistral's poem masks a very sophisticated technique largely inspired by the decasyllabic poetry of Dante. The French Academy awarded the poem the Née Prize.

Mistral then formed the project of founding a museum dedicated to Provence and chose Arles, the ancient capital, for its location. It was first housed on the third floor of the Justice Hall and was later transfered to the Palais Royal. The Museon Arlaten opened its doors in 1896 with exhibits devoted to the history, art and customs of Provence. Mistral

also continued to write stories, often under various pseudonyms, but *L'Aïoli* was in trouble and neglected by Marieton and his friends.[27] Around this time, Mistral's health began to show signs of age. Suffering from a persistent eczema, his doctor sent him for treatment to Vacqueyras, town of the famous troubadour. Then a period of depression set in following the subsequent deaths of his dear friends Mathieu, Arène, Daudet, Gras and Balaguer. Of the old guard only Tavan remained. The latter had recently published a comedy (*Li masc,* 1897) and shortly before his death, in 1905, *Vido Vivanto.*

In 1904, Mistral received the Nobel Prize for literature together with José Echegaray and immediately invested the sum in his museum. He then worked on his memoirs (*Memori e Raconte*, 1906), a Provençal translation of Genesis (*La Genèsi,* 1910), and prepared a collection of poems (1880–1912) which he published with the title *Lis Oulivado* (1912). He spent the last years of his life at home with his wife. Mornings were devoted to correspondence and afternoons to walks or entertaining guests such as young Henri Bosco, or President Henri Poincaré. Mistral would often drop by at Roumanille's bookshop in Avignon but he spent most of his time in the Museon Arlaten working on his collections. As the years went by, the old poet felt more and more isolated. Now the vast majority of the first generation of *Félibres* had passed away. Alexandrine Gautier (*Li Blavet de Mountmajour, Velo Blanco*) died in 1898, Rémy Marcellin (*Long dou Camin)* in 1908, and Eugène Plauchud (*Lou Diamant de Sant-Maime)* in 1909.

Fortunately Mistral had inspired a host of younger writers including Batisto Bonnet (*Vido D'Enfant, Lou Carpan)* and Charloun Rieu (*Li Cant dou Terraire*, 1897*)* who took an active part in the movement or contributed to the literary tradition with their poems, novels and short stories. In 1913, Mistral attended, for the last time, the festival of Sainte Estelle in Aix. He died at home on March 25, 1914, and according to his last wish, was buried in his backyard. His wife, much younger, lived in the shadow of the poet in their home until her death in 1943.

Endnotes

1. Cited by Emile Ripert, *La Renaissance Provençale: 1800–1860* (Marseilles: Laffitte Reprints, 1978) 142.

2. "Je suis devenu amoureux, aux environs de Buoux, d'une femme qui fait très bien les omelettes à l'huile, a de fort beaux yeux et ne sait pas un mot de

français.... Les natifs ne savent ni ne comprennent le français" Prosper Mérimée, *Correspondance Générale* 17 vols. (Paris: Le Divan 1941–1964) I:335.

3. "L'ancienne littérature provençale n'est pas seulement la première en date des littératures de l'Europe moderne, c'est celle qui a agi le plus tôt et le plus longtemps sur la plupart des autres, qui leur a donné le plus de son esprit et de ses formes et dont l'histoire tient le plus à la leur." Ripert, *La Renaissance Provençale* 83.

4. "La monstrueuse guerre des Albigeois qui détruisit la civilisation du Midi porta aussi un coup mortel à sa littérature." Ripert 85.

5. "Avant trente ans cette langue sera aussi difficile à expliquer que la langue des hyérogliphes." Lucien Gaillard, *Victor Gélu: Poète du Peuple marseillais* (Marseilles: Laffitte, 1985) 93.

6. Frédéric Mistral, *Memori e Raconte* (Raphèle-lès-Arles: Marcel Petit, 1980) 3.

7. Claude Mauron, *Frédéric Mistral* (Paris: Fayard, 1993).

8. Jacques-Henry Bornecque, *Les Années d'Apprentissage d'Alphonse Daudet* (Paris: Nizet, 1951) 281.

9. Mistral, *Memori e Raconte* 23.

10. Henri Moucadel, *Maillane: le temps retrouvé* (Marguerittes: Equinoxes, 1992) 61.

11. René Dumas, *Les Années de Formation de Joseph Roumanille 1818–1848* (Paris: Sorbonne, Thèse d'Etat, 1970) 148.

12. Mistral, *Memori e Raconte* 105.

13. Mistral 111.

14. René Jouveau, *Histoire du Félibrige* 4 vols. (Aix-en-Provence, 1984) I: 65.

15. Jouveau 66.

16. Jouveau 81–81

17. Jouveau 76.

18. For this information I am indebted to Laurent Aubanel, great-grandson of the poet who to this day continues the family business and tradition.

19. "Je vous remercie, Monsieur, d'avoir pensé à moi. Votre poème est beau, très beau, et charmant, plein de grandeur, d'originalité et de charme. Je l'ai lu avec le plus vif plaisir et je salue de coeur un des premiers poètes, selon moi, de la France." *Correspondance de George Sand,* ed. Georges Lubin 25 vols. (Paris: Garnier 1964–91) XV: 347–48.

20. Charles Rostaing, *Mistral: l'Homme révélé par ses oeuvres* (Marseilles:Laffitte, 1987) 33.

21. Jouveau, *Histoire du Félibrige* I: 158.

22. Jouveau 192.

23. Fréderic Mistral, *Calendau: Pouèmo nouvèu* (Avignon: Roumanille, 1867) 157.

24. "Le félibrige est né sous les arbres, il vit en plein air depuis trente ans, et j'ai bien peur du tapis vert académique." Marie Dumon-Legré and Pierre Legré, *Un Humaniste du XIXe siècle: Ludovic Legré* (Marseilles: Laffitte, 1982) 48.

25. Mistral, *Lou Poèmo dou Rose* (Paris: Lemerre, 1897) 6.

26. Mistral 8.

27. "Je fais mon possible pour que tout soit bouclé et pour que la barque suive son cours, depuis huit ans. Mais je ne peux pas tout faire. Pauvre Félibrige, les hommes s'y font rare." Mauron, *Mistral* 318.

Three

Alphonse Daudet

Alphonse Daudet was born just on the other side of the Rhône, in Nîmes, on May 13, 1840. His family came from the small village of Concoules, further north in the Cévennes mountains, where his great-grandparents were peasants and his grandfather Jacques Daudet worked in the silk business. In 1829, Jacques' son Vincent married twenty-four-year-old Adeline Reynaud from Nîmes and settled there. The Reynauds were also in the silk trade. They had their roots in the Ardèche region, a little above the town of Alès and were all good Catholics and royalists. The marriage was a happy one and Adeline gave birth to three sons and a daughter. The children grew up in a middle-class home with a father devoted to his scarf business and a romantic mother with a passion for literature. Nîmes at the time was a booming town of about fifty-five thousand people whose economy revolved around silk. Politically it was divided between the partisans of Henry V, son of the exiled king Charles X and direct heir to the throne, the Orleanists who supported

Alphonse Daudet 1840–1897 (Photograph Palais du Roure, Avignon).

the current King Louis Philippe, and the Republicans. For more than a century, the region had also been the seat of many bloody battles between Catholics and Protestants and no one had forgotten their devastating effects.

Daudet's family was Catholic and legitimist. According to his family, Mr. Daudet would not decorate the walls of his house until the royal heir had returned to the throne. They lived in town but their small factory was on the road to Avignon. Unfortunately, Alphonse was born at a time when the town's economy was in crisis, which affected Mr. Daudet's business. Competition (especially for wool) was fierce, and water, necessary for the dyeing process, was no longer as abundant as in the past, and Mr. Daudet had difficulty maintaining a good income. Alphonse was a handsome child, with his dark curly hair and brown eyes, but he was also very nearsighted and his health was fragile, so his parents sent him to live on a farm a few miles outside of town in the small village of Bezouce, in the direction of Avignon. Daudet's host family was the Trinquiés, their maid's parents. They raised Alphonse as best they could and he shared the life of country people, played in the fields, helped in the garden, fed the animals and, to his father's dismay, learned to speak Provençal! "In Bezouce," Daudet would later remember, "I was in harmony with the people, I shared their lives, their games, their tales and songs. I was intoxicated by the divine must of our language."[1] As Alain Gérard remarks, from that time on Daudet's love for Provence remained deeply rooted.[2]

Daudet's health improved and when he was six he was returned to his family, for school awaited him. In 1846, his parents sent him to a

religious institution, *Les Frères de La Doctrine Chrétienne* and then, in 1848, to the *Pension Canivet*. The contrast between the happy days spent in close contact with nature and the restrictive atmosphere of the school must have been brutal, for it left some bitterness in his memories. The school's buildings were dark and humid, and the teachers very strict. "We recited our lessons on our knees," Daudet wrote in *Numa Roumestan*. Young Alphonse struggled through Latin and learned mathematics with great difficulty, for his mind was elsewhere. At home, whenever he had the time to borrow books from the library, he devoured *Robinson Crusoe* and *Tom Jones*. From time to time, his father would take him to the factory and Daudet, fascinated, would spend hours watching the workers turn raw silk into colorful ribbons and scarves. He loved to hide behind the machines, make forts and play Robinson Crusoe. The factory had become one of his favorite playgrounds! Sometimes he would also stop by his uncle's pharmacy and observe the assistants crushing and mixing together hundreds of different herbs and plants of various colors and aromas. On market days, Daudet would make sure to wake up early to accompany his father to the town of Beaucaire.

The year 1848 was a tragic one for the Daudets. The revolution established a new Socialist republic which made a return of Henry V very unlikely even in the near future. Then the family business went through a series of crisis. First, they lost their most important customer, then an employee strike paralyzed their activity and finally, dissatisfied dye-sellers filed a lawsuit against the company. Mr. Daudet, bankrupt, sold the business, and, in the spring of 1849, moved his family, with a new baby girl, to Lyons, a leading center of the silk trade. To young Alphonse, the news came as a terrible blow. "It seemed as if the sky came tumbling down ... what about my island! My caves! My forts!," he later wrote in *Le Petit Chose*.[3]

Daudet always remembered the seven years spent in Lyons as the worst of his life. Not only were the Daudets exiles but, in the days of slow travel and poor communications, as Jacques Rouré reminds us, Lyons felt further north than it does now and was almost a foreign land.[4] After sailing up the Rhône River for a few days, the family finally arrived in their new city and rented an apartment alongside the river. The boys were soon sent off to school, first to a small Catholic institution and later, with the help of scholarships, to the *Lycée Ampère*. Alphonse's lack of interest in school did not improve and his vivid imagination often led him astray to the banks of the river, where he sipped

glasses of wine with his friends in secret hideaways or canoed alone on the Rhône in search of a desert island. From this point on, his love for water began which he shared with his fellow-writers Pierre Loti and Guy de Maupassant. The long and cold winters, accompanied by fog and rain, not to mention gray skies filled with factory smoke, stood in sharp contrast to the dry and sunny South. Their maid, overcome with depression, had already returned home. But the climatic conditions were not the only problem and Daudet's Lyonnais schoolmates often mocked his pronunciation and Southern accent. Daily existence turned into a veritable nightmare. Daudet withdrew from social activities and entered a phase of gloom and depression. To make things worse, his older brother Henri contracted meningitis and died. Things changed when, one day, as he later told Mistral, he discovered a copy of *L'Armana Provençau*. Daudet immediately took his pen and began to write verse in Provençal.

Fortunately, the Daudets' stay in Lyons came to an end in 1857 when Mr. Daudet accepted a new position in Brittany. The family did not follow him there and Alphonse saw his father only on rare occasions after his departure. Mrs. Daudet and her daughter returned to live with their uncle, while Ernest found a position with a Parisian publisher. Alphonse had not completed his studies, his parents not being able to afford to pay for his last year, but a relative of his managed to find work for him in a school in Alès, at the foot of the Cévennes, " narrow valley, completely encircled by a wall of mountains."[5] His duties at school included the care of the younger students during recess, and overnight in the dormitory. Little is known of his actual living conditions in Alès and the version given in his story *Le Petit Chose*, is closer to fiction than to reality according to most scholars. It is not known if, as Daniel Eyssette, the young protagonist of the story, Daudet actually had a fight with one of his older students, the son of an influential and well-known Marquis, or if he was relieved of his functions for writing love letters to the underprefect's maid, nor do we know if there was any link between Daniel's suicide attempt and Daudet. It seems certain though that Daudet was, for many reasons, dissatisfied with his job, in a school where the majority of students spoke, despite the law, a Cévenol dialect bewildering to Daudet. So, when he received a letter from his brother Ernest inviting him to Paris, he seized the opportunity to escape his bleak future, and after four months of a tedious and boring job, he left for the capital. Knowing his imaginative mind and his burning desire for adventure and, perhaps, literary ambitions, he must have been elated. On a cold night of November 1857, Daudet, not yet eighteen, arrived in Paris.

Ernest now worked for the newspaper *Le Spectateur* and lived at 7 Rue de Tournon, in a small apartment next to the future politician Léon Gambetta, a law student at the time. In 1859, the two brothers moved to Rue Bonaparte, near the Saint-Germain-des-Prés church and later Alphonse lived alone in L'Allée des Veuves. During his years of apprenticeship in Paris, Daudet earned his living as a freelance journalist, writing articles on the arts and letters for newspapers and magazines such a *Le Figaro,* and *Le Journal Illustré.* He lived in the bohemian manner of artists, frequented their cafés, discussed art in Montmartre with destitute painters, and drank *absinthe* with poets Charles Bataille, Amédée Roland, Baudelaire and then later Verlaine. Occasionally he was introduced into more fashionable literary salons such as those of Louise Colet, Madame Chodsko and Countess LaTrémoille. In spite of his fragile health, Daudet was a sensual man. His first serious love interest seems to have been Marie Rieu, a model with whom he lived for some time. When he was not in the cafés or writing book reviews, Daudet composed poems, which he first published as a collection in 1858 with the title *Les Amoureuses.* Although largely ignored by the press, his book nevertheless succeeded in attracting the attention of Empress Eugénie who asked to meet him. Daudet was proud and the interview proved fruitful, for the Empress obtained an administrative position for him with the Duke of Morny, Emperor Napoléon III's stepbrother and President of the Legislative Assembly. Daudet was elated with his new position that not only provided him with a good steady income but also left him enough time to pursue his literary interests. Furthermore, Daudet and Morny quickly became good friends.

In the early 1860s, Daudet often met with a group of Provençal poets including Eugène Garcin and Pierre Véron. They discussed literature and especially Mistral. Daudet himself had loved *Mireio* and met Mistral in April 1859, when the latter came to Paris to promote his book. Daudet was "irresistibly drawn to him" because, as he confessed, Mistral recited his poetry in Provençal, "the language that my father forbade me to speak!"[6] Mistral was only too pleased to meet a man with whom he could converse in Provençal and accepted Daudet's invitation with pleasure. Over dinner at Daudet's apartment, a lifelong friendship between the two men was born. "When he spoke," Daudet later remembered, "a sweet, fresh and powerful fragrance of the country I had long ago abandoned, filled the tiny room and through this wonderful, clear and musical language, Provence came alive again, in a corner of Paris."[7] The following year, Daudet spent his summer in Maillane at the Mistrals'

home and together the two friends toured the country. Mistral was only too proud to show Daudet around. They attended summer festivals, read poetry under pine trees, picked grapes in the fields, tasted local dishes and wines, and above all enjoyed conversing in the vernacular with each other and with the villagers at the terrace of shady cafés. Daudet had never felt happier in his life and took the train back to Paris full of vivid emotions and memories.

But in the meantime, his brother Ernest had left Paris to take up a better position in Blois, and Daudet found himself alone. He enjoyed his work but inspired by Mistral's success spent more time at his desk, writing stories. In the next couple of years he published two novels *La Double Conversion* (1861), *Le Roman du Chaperon Rouge* (1862) and a play, *La Dernière Idole* (1863), but unfortunately Parisian critics and artists alike continued to ignore him. At that time, Daudet's fragile health, affected by years of cold, damp Parisian winters and alcohol abuse, began to show signs of deterioration. His doctor, fearing the worst, ordered rest and recommended a stay in more Southern climes.

Thus Daudet began to travel, beginning with his native Midi. After a visit to his mother in Nîmes and to Mistral in Maillane, Daudet and his cousin Henri Reynaud left for the French colony of Algeria, at the time a fashionable place for romantic artists in search of exotic flavors. There he enjoyed two months of sunny weather, visited Algiers and ventured even further south into the desert. He was fascinated with the new scenery and especially with its fauna and flora but also observed the sharp contrast between the exuberant lifestyle of the French colonists and the impenetrable world of the Arabs. After a brief return to Paris, Daudet left again, for the island of Corsica in the winter of 1864. There, he traveled along the coast stopping at villages and listening attentively to their fishermen's tales. He also went inland to the remote mountain hamlets, tasted their cheese and recorded the legends of their shepherds. Again Daudet recovered his physical and mental health.

He spent the summer of 1864 in Provence at his aunt's estate of Montauban near the village of Fontvieille, a few miles south of Maillane. Daudet always felt at home there and he loved his dear aunt and the stories of her childhood. Mistral's home being only a couple of miles away, Daudet often crossed the fields to Maillane, a walking stick in one hand and his inseparable Montaigne in the other, to the *maison du lézard*, "the last house on the left on the road to Saint-Rémy."[8] Mistral always received Daudet like a brother and in order not to bother his old mother, the two shared a bedroom in the attic. Again they conversed in

Provençal, told each other stories, caroused in the cafés until dawn, visited Les Baux, Beaucaire, and camped in Camargue. Daudet had met Mistral's friends and was soon adopted by the joyous *Félibres* and drank Mathieu's homemade red wine. Mistral and his companions took Daudet to Arles' Roman ruins and old abbey of Mont-Majour, and they all danced and courted many a young *chato* of Avignon. Yet it was in the quiet atmosphere of an abandoned windmill near Fontvieille, surrounded with lavender fields, that Daudet found his inspiration. Daudet considered himself a *Félibre* at heart and then signed his poems by the name *Félibre de la tour du Brau.*[9] In turn the Provençal poets accepted Daudet as one of them. Along with *Mireio,* Daudet always carried a copy of Aubanel's *Miougrano.*

Back in Paris, the situation changed for the worse since, following Morny's death in 1865, Daudet lost his job. He then resumed his bohemian lifestyle and for some time resided in an artist colony in Clamart outside Paris, and eked out a mere living writing reviews and articles for the press. Whenever he felt depressed and lonely he took the train for Provence where he found a refuge in an abandoned windmill near Fontvieille. There, sheltered from the vibrant sun and intoxicated with the fragrance of thyme and lavender, he found his inspiration and when he returned to Paris his ears were still ringing with the songs, laughter, and magic of the land. Daudet turned over a new leaf and began to write about Provence.[10]

In December 1865, during the performance of Goncourt's *Henriette Maréchal,* Daudet met Julia Allard, daughter of a rich Parisian cabinetmaker. Julia was not especially pretty but her good upbringing and manners attracted him and she, in turn, could not resist his long black hair and melancholy eyes. Julia's mother Léonide, herself a close friend of poetess Marcelline Desbordes-Valmore, held a literary salon where writers Barbey D'Aurevilly and François Coppée were often seen. Encouraged by her mother, Julia had published some poetry under the pseudonym of Marguerite Tournay. Daudet and Julia fell in love, but the Allards were republicans and courting Julia was not an easy task for Daudet. But Julia was so in love that Mr. Allard finally consented to the marriage and the ceremony took place in January 1867, in the church Saint Denis-du-Sacrement with Mistral, in Paris for the publication of *Calendau,* as best man.

For their honeymoon, the couple traveled south to Provence where they visited his cousins the Ambroys, moved on to Cassis, and went back to Maillane to greet Mistral and his friends. Julia was a Parisian and

never felt completely at home in Provence, not to mention that she was also a little jealous of her husband's friendship with Mistral. Mistral himself was polite and courteous toward her but could not understand Daudet's attraction to her. On the contrary, Edmond de Goncourt, who later became a good friend of the family's, was fascinated by Julia's charm and her artistic talent, and in his *Journal* he describes her as a truly remarkable woman and devoted wife. Daudet was aware of his wife's qualities and, despite his numerous affairs, he remained close to her all of his life. Julia was forgiving and generous. She often helped him with his stories and he in turn always accepted her literary advice without hesitation. The Daudets moved into an apartment in the Marais and in 1867, Léon, their first son was born.

The following year, the Daudets began to spend their summers in Champrosay, a charming little village southeast of Paris, near Draveil, where the Allards were renting a large house, formerly occupied by painter Eugène Delacroix. It was located near the Seine and the Sénart Forest and was only an hour away from Paris. Daudet's mother had by then joined her husband in Paris where Ernest's wife and child were also living. Daudet's early married life was difficult for money was scarce. He wrote profusely but without much success and Julia was often forced to pawn her jewelry or to ask her father for help. However, with the publication of *Le Petit Chose* (1868), that first appeared serially in *Le Moniteur Universel,* there was hope for the future. Reviews were favorable and Daudet suddenly emerged as a promising novelist. The tale was realistic and largely autobiographical, which explained in part its small success. It is the story of Daniel Eyssette, a Provençal who grows up in Lyons and tells of his miserable school days. The plot is very simple but the portraits of some of the characters, such as the pipe-smoking priest and Bamban the dirty and lame student, are picturesque and masterly drawn. Unlike Balzac's stories, Daudet's tale is not burdened with unnecessary details and reminds the reader more of Mark Twain, who was one of his favorite authors. Daudet also showed that he could entertain the reader with more dramatic events such as Daniel's fight with Boucoyran, one of his students and the son of an influential notable, and his dismissal from the school after the principal discovered love letters Daniel wrote to help his friend Roger and mistakenly attributed to him. As it was told in simple language and from the point of view of a young man, Daudet's story became a textbook for school children in the next century. However, the style was still hesitant and awkward at times.

Daudet now saw his friend Paul Arène quite often. Arène was a jovial Provençal exile who, like Daudet, was trying to make it as a writer. Light, lithe and of small stature, with a distinguished pointy beard and a dark but warm complexion, he looked like a Greek goatherd.[11] A native of Sisteron, where he was born three years later than Daudet, Arène was the son of a watchmaker and a milliner. His school days in the *Collège des Frères* of the town were happier than Daudet's and Arène enjoyed reading the classics and particularly Horace and Virgil. He later attended the University of Aix where he majored in Philosophy and then spent a year in Marseilles, teaching. Arène made the acquaintance of Roumanille, Tavan and Mistral, shortly before obtaining his *licence* in 1863. The following year Arène was transferred to the *Lycée Impérial* (now Michelet) in Vanves, near Paris.

Paul Arène 1843–1896 (Photograph Palais du Roure, Avignon).

But Vanves was too small and boring for a young man and Arène spent a lot of time in Paris where he frequented the Café de Madrid, Boulevard Montmartre, and Bobino in the Latin Quarter. It was there, sitting in a crowded room filled with smoke and drunken artists that Arène loved to write and where he met Alfred Delvau, Charles Bataille, Jules Vallès and Daudet. Arène made a meager living writing articles for newspapers such as *Le Nain Jaune, Le Masque* and *Le Figaro.* He dreamed of becoming a famous playwright. He corresponded with Mistral, Aubanel and Roumanille, and lived in Clamart with Daudet, Bataille and Jean Duboys. Arène had more luck than Daudet did and his play *Pierrot Héritier,* a tragedy played at the Odéon Theater in

October 1865, was quite a success. Shortly afterwards he resigned his teaching position and devoted his time to literature.

Daudet and Arène had cooperated on a series of letters about Provence, which appeared in *L'Evénement* and *Le Figaro* in 1866. They were entitled *Lettres de mon Moulin* and signed with the pseudonym Marie-Gaston, a character from Balzac. Marie was Daudet and behind Gaston hid Arène. The tales were collected into a book and published by Hetzel in 1869 with Daudet's name only, Julia Daudet's idea, according to Arène. Success was not immediate and according to Daudet, "the two thousand copies sold with difficulty,"[12] but over the years, the book became a bestseller and a classic. It is difficult to determine the specific role that each played in the writing of the tales. Daudet often said Arène wrote the best ones, which the latter politely refused to admit. Yet Arène's share should not be underestimated for he too was a born storyteller and during his lifetime wrote several hundred stories. It seems, however, that in this case, Daudet had written more than Arène. These letters, supposedly written from the windmill of Fontvieille "a thousand leagues from Parisian fog, on a sunny hill, in the country of tambourine and Muscat wine", reveal their common love of Provence.[13] The narratives are simple and the style always poetic, with here and there just a touch of Provençal language. Like Willa Cather, Henry James succumbed to the "extraordinary charm" of the book and said of Daudet that he was "an admirable genius…at the head of his profession."[14]

In the *Lettres de mon Moulin,* the authors speak of their Provence with a definite pride and a certain amount of nostalgia which gives the book a melancholy tone at times. Provence is a land where "springs sing clearer than elsewhere" and "mountain spirits come and go freely." There in the imperturbable silence one can hear "rustles in the air" and "hear the grass grow."[15] Nostalgia is almost omnipresent but especially marked in tales such as "Installation" and "The Stars" where they recall the good old days when people lived simply and in harmony with one another. But these tales also contain humor, Daudet's distinctive mark. Unlike Mistral, Daudet does not hesitate to mock the Provençals and tales such as "The Pope's mule," "The Vicar of Cucugnan" and "Father Gaucher's elixir" certainly anticipate his *Tartarin.*

Besides humor, the dominant tone of the tales is melancholy and the story of Blanquette, Mr. Seguin's goat, is particularly moving. Blanquette who, eager to be free, escapes the security and comfort of the farm, and enjoys a few hours of happiness in the fields to find herself alone when darkness came and in the presence of a ferocious and

starving wolf. Mr. Seguin's goat fought back until dawn when exhausted she let herself be devoured. Was Blanquette symbolic of the destiny of the Provençal artist in exile? "Master Cornille's secret" is another classic tale that illustrates the problems engendered by the Industrial Revolution. Cornille is the last miller of his village whose once booming activity has recently been brought to an end by the installation of a modern factory. However, out of pride, Cornille continues to work, which in the absence of customers is very mysterious. One day, someone finds out that the sacks he is carrying are actually filled with plaster. Dismayed and saddened the villagers begin to help Cornille out and take their cereal to his mill again, thus saving his life and restoring their ancestral tradition. Particularly moving is "The Old People" a tale about the misery of old age and "The Woman from Arles" which tells of Jan's impossible love story and subsequent suicide. Daudet's poetic touch, illustrated by these beautiful tales, deeply moved Mistral who compared him to an elf that makes everything he touches sparkle and shine."[16]

Now that Daudet was married, Arène saw him less often and whenever he felt homesick he would take the train and head back to Sisteron to visit his parents and younger siblings. During the summer of 1868, Arène fell in love with Anaïs Roumieux of Beaucaire, a friend of the *Félibres*. Arène proposed but, unfortunately, Mr. Roumieux disapproved and his daughter did not defy him. Daudet comforted him as best he could and helped him with *Jean des Figues* (1868), the story of a Provençal poet and his adventures in the capital. Daudet himself continued to sharpen his art with a new story *Tartarin de Tarascon* (1872). Previously serialized in *Le Petit Moniteur* and *Le Figaro, Tartarin* is a comic tale inspired in its form and content from Cervantes. Its protagonist Tartarin, as Daudet himself tells us, is a mixture of Don Quixote and Sancho Panza, and there lies its originality and humor. Tartarin has Quixote's vivid imagination but Panza's body. He is a middle-aged bachelor who has never left his hometown of Tarascon on the Rhône but grows baobabs in his garden and decorates his house with exotic memorabilia, such as Caribbean arrows, Corsican knives and Malaysian daggers. He also possesses a rich library where he likes to peruse Cook's voyages and other exotic tales of men hunting elephants or bears. The arrival of a circus with real lions to this peaceful little town of Tarascon reawakens Tartarin's hunter spirit and, encouraged by the villagers who always considered him somewhat of a hero, he promises to go lion hunting in Africa. Most of the tale takes place in Algeria and Daudet relied on his travels there to give the tale a realistic touch of local color.

Needless to say Tartarin's adventures in North Africa are entertaining and amusing. After a rough crossing of the Mediterranean Sea, which kept him to his bed, Tartarin, dressed as a veritable warrior and armed to his teeth, finally lands in North Africa. Impatient for action and finding the city with sidewalk cafés and French colonists too civilized for his taste, Tartarin quickly ventures alone into the back country and after lying in ambush all night, shoots an approaching animal which, at dawn, turns out to be a donkey. His stay in Algeria is, in fact, a long series of misfortunes. Swindled by a prostitute, he is later robbed by her pimp. Then, Tartarin accidentally kills a circus lion and is on the verge of being lynched by the population when he is finally rescued by the Provençal ship captain who takes him back to Tarascon where he is received with honors. If Cervante's novel and the picaresque genre inspired Daudet, Tartarin is also a caricature of Provençal men, and to some extent, as Murray Sachs noted, of Daudet himself.[17] Flaubert declared the book a masterpiece and told Daudet that he burst out laughing several times.[18] But back in Tarascon, *Tartarin* had caused a great scandal and the population, offended by his grotesque caricatures of Provençals, swore vengeance, and, years later, when he and Mistral visited the town, they were received with insults and shotguns.

War with Prussia and the chaos that ensued temporarily stopped Daudet's literary activity. When the hostilities began on July 15, 1870, Daudet was still recuperating from a boating accident in which he broke his leg. Arène had joined the army in Lyons. On September 2, 1870 Napoleon III surrendered but, on the 4th, Parisians proclaimed France a Republic and resumed the defense of the capital. There followed a five-month siege, which lasted until January 28, 1871 when, exhausted and famished, they finally capitulated. The elections of February 8th gave a large majority to the monarchists, which caused some republicans to rebel and to create a *Commune*. By the Treaty of Frankfurt (May 10, 1871), France lost Alsace and part of Lorraine to Prussia, which occupied the country until 1873.

Like his contemporaries, Daudet was profoundly affected by these events. His leg injury had prevented him from taking part in the battle, but, during the siege, Daudet joined the National Guards and participated actively in the defense of the city, refusing, however, to fight against the *Communards*. In April, he and his family left Paris for Champrosay where Daudet's father-in-law had bought a house in 1868. Daudet's imagination took a sharp turn and there, in the relative peace of the country, he documented his experiences of the recent events in

the form of articles published in *Le Soir* or *L'Evénement.* These were later collected in a series of books such as *Lettres à un Absent* (1871), *Contes du Lundi* (1873) and *Robert Helmont* (1874). Most of these tales contain realistic portraits of the horrors of war and of the chaos engendered by the siege: houses transformed into bunkers, obsession with spies, arrests of foreigners, famine and the killing of zoo animals for food. Daudet made sure to mention the acts of courage and heroism of some and the treason of others, pointing all along to the futility and the absurdity of wars. He later confided to Goncourt that war had made him realize he could die a relatively unknown writer, which encouraged him to work harder.[19]

Daudet was now in his mid-thirties. Family life, the war, and the political turn of events had changed him. He had become more mature but also more pessimistic. His bohemian habits and friends were now a thing of the past, except perhaps his love of beautiful women. Since he had little luck with his tales he now turned to the theater, but his plays *Le Sacrifice* (1869) and *Lise Tavernier* (1869) unfortunately failed to attract the attention of the public. In 1872, he tried again with *L'Arlésienne* with music by Georges Bizet and performed at the Théâtre du Vaudeville. The story, set in western Provence, tells of the tragic love of Frédéri Mamaï for with a lady from Arles. Frédéri managed to convince his family to consent to the union but in the midst of the marriage preparations Mitifio appears with disruptive news. Mitifio informs Francet Mamaï, Frédéri's grandfather, that the lady from Arles has been his mistress for two years and shows her love letters which he leaves with him. Francet explains the tragic situation to his widowed daughter-in-law Rose and Balthazar his shepherd, and shows Frédéri the letters. Frédéri is disheartened but as time passes, he manages to get back on his feet and agrees to marry Vivette, a childhood friend who is in love with him. However, in the meantime, Mitifio, looking for his letters, surfaces again and by chance meets Frédéri, and the two talk about the Lady from Arles again. The same night, haunted by the ghost of his former love, Frédéri throws himself out of the attic window. Zola enjoyed the play, which according to him seemed to have all the necessary ingredients for success: a good plot, romantic passion, a touch of local folklore, and music by talented Bizet. But, as Mistral had foreseen, it nevertheless failed to attract the Parisians and ended after only eight performances.

After the war and the *Commune,* Arène came back to Paris and was warmly received by the Daudets. Arène still wrote for the theater

(*Un Duel aux Lanternes*, *L'Ilote*) but with no more success than Daudet
and continued to contribute literary criticism for *La République
Française* and numerous tales for *Gil Blas* and *L'Echo de Paris*. Like
Daudet, he had remained in contact with the *Félibres* and wrote poems
in Provençal for *L'Armana*. As soon as he had some time off he would
travel to Provence and join his friends in their festivities. For the Daudets
as well literary success was decidedly hard to come by and both Julia
and Alphonse resorted to work as literary critics for his brother Ernest,
now director of the *Journal Officiel*. Their new position was to have a
great impact on their lives and careers, for it put them in the middle of
the art scene and introduced them to a circle of established writers such
as Flaubert, Zola, and Goncourt who unanimously adopted the couple.
Daudet's new friends gave him the support and encouragement he
needed.

Flaubert had enjoyed *Le Petit Chose* and recommended Daudet to
George Sand, urging her to begin with *Tartarin*.[20] Zola knew Daudet
from his early days as literary critic for *L'Evénement*, and as for
Goncourt, eighteen years older, Daudet reminded him of his recently
departed brother Jules. At first he criticized Daudet's exuberance and
style, which he found too simple, but over the years, his opinion greatly
improved and the two became inseparable friends. Goncourt had also a
great admiration for Julia's artistic talent. She, in turn, found in him a
confidant and mentor who encouraged her to write from her inner soul
and to express her femininity. On April 14, 1874, the group, including
Daudet, baptized themselves "Les Auteurs Sifflés" (The Booed Authors),
a title chosen because of their common failure in the theater, and began
to meet regularly for dinner at Brébant's or Riche's. They soon adopted
Russian writer Ivan Turgenev who swore he was booed in his own country.[21] When not dining together in town, they would visit each other, at
Flaubert's on Sundays or Zola's house in Médan. Daudet entertained
his friends at home on Thursdays and Goncourt in his *grenier* in Auteuil.
With them Daudet learned the art of realistic literature and their lessons
soon bore fruit. "Lisez donc *Fromont et Risler* de mon ami Daudet,"
Flaubert wrote Sand in 1874.[22]

Daudet's new novel finally brought him the long-awaited success
and both critics and Parisian readers praised it. The story takes place in
Paris and tells of unhappy love affairs. Guillaume Risler, the protagonist, marries Sidonie, in spite of her having recently been courted by
his younger brother Frantz. Désirée on the other hand, loves Frantz.
Risler's marriage is unhappy and Sidonie has several lovers including

Georges Fromont, the new manager of the factory for which Risler works. Fromont borrows company money to offer Sidonie presents, which slowly brings the company to the brink of collapse. Risler finally learns about his wife's infidelities and confronts Sidonie who admits that she has always been in love with his brother. Astounded by the news and disillusioned with life, Risler hangs himself. The book was a huge success and was praised by Zola who declared that he had rarely read so moving and delightful a story.[23] Daudet's son Lucien remembered how his father went to his publisher Charpentier, asked to be paid in gold coins and in an uncontrollable display of joy dumped them in the middle of the living room, in front of Julia, equally elated.

To Daudet and the other members of the group, their dinner gatherings were sacred, not only because they were the occasion of literary discussions, but also because they were all *bons vivants,* all enjoyed gourmet meals and fine wines. *Bouillabaisse* was often ordered in Daudet's honor and Turgenev would never miss a chance to bring caviar back from Russia. These parties were also jovial and certainly reminded Daudet of Mistral and the merrymaking *Félibres.* After a few glasses of wine Daudet was known to evoke his beloved Provence, and Maupassant, often a guest, would entertain the group with his latest love affairs. Weekends were spent sometimes at Flaubert's in Croisset, near Rouen, or in Champrosay, where Daudet, Arène and Goncourt would take long walks in the Sénart Forest to *L'Ermitage* and pay a visit to their photographer friend Nadar. Daudet had finally found his niche and the friends he needed to become a successful writer, and he continued to follow their advice.

His new novel, *Jack* (1876), was also a success and received the Jouy Prize. Reminiscent of Dickens's *Great Expectations, Jack* tells the story of an illegitimate young boy abandoned to his fate by a mother, a poor and frivolous woman obsessed with wealth and social status. After being a border at a mediocre school crowded with African students, Jack manages to escape and to join his mother living outside Paris with Argenson, the school's former professor of literature, an arrogant and insensitive fellow, concerned only with himself and his poetry. Over the years, Argenton grows weary of Jack and decides to send him to a factory to teach him a trade and make a worker out of him. Thus Jack labors in a steel manufacture for some time until he is wrongly accused of theft and loses his job. He then spends a couple of years on a ship working as a mechanic but unfortunately the ship sinks, and Jack goes back to live with his mother again. There he falls in love with his

childhood friend Cécile, raised by her grandparents after the death of her unwed mother, but his finances do not allow him to stay there and he leaves for Paris to earn a living. His mother comes and visits him but alas too late for Jack, who has contracted tuberculosis, dies in her arms.

Zola praised the novel for its naturalistic style and especially enjoyed the descriptions of factory labor and the workers' poor living conditions. "It's the best novel you've written so far!" he wrote him shortly after the publication.[24] Zola was right and, looking back, Daudet's novel has indeed all the characteristics (and defects) of the novels in vogue, namely an overabundance of characters and adventures and, above all, too pervasive a sentimentality. Motherhood is also a central theme but the son's constant yearning for his mother could be interpreted in a symbolic way, as Daudet's own desire to be in Provence. Daudet's contemporaries enjoyed the book. Mistral found it moving and full of charm. Flaubert praised it but reproached Daudet for condescending a little too much to the vogue. Again, he sent a copy to Sand and invited her to make Daudet's acquaintance.[25] *Jack* was later adapted for the theater and performed for the first time at the Odéon in 1881.[26] With fame Daudet began to earn a good income and the family moved to Place des Vosges, a more respectable neighborhood. Julia initiated weekly dinners and invited new acquaintances such as painter Auguste Renoir. Encouraged by his recent success, Daudet imposed on himself a rigorous schedule, got up at four o'clock in the morning and wrote most of the day in his attic room. Unfortunately, the long hours spent at his desk, combined with a lack of physical exercise and too much wine undermined his health and soon his former problems resurfaced. In 1876, he suffered his first heart attack.

Daudet paid attention to Flaubert's criticism and his next novel, *Le Nabab* (1877), is free of some of the unnecessary details and sentimentalism of his former one. It remains, however, "un tableau de moeurs parisiennes," and describes, in the manner of his realist friends, the petty political intrigues and love affairs of the Parisian middle and upper classes of the 1860s, a world where new wealth challenged class values and traditions. But this time the protagonists are Provençals. Native of Bourg-St-Andéol, near Montélimar, where he was born into a poor family, Jansoulet moved to Paris with his wife and children after twenty years in Tunisia, where he assembled a large fortune. Jansoulet's ambition is to enter the world of politics and to be elected as a representative in the National Assembly. The story is about ambition and greed, and shows how

Jansoulet's political enemies, jealous of his fortune, cooperate and plot against him to cause his downfall. Betrayed by his friends Jansoulet dies, ruined and broken-hearted. The novel was a success but Goncourt, a little jealous of the popularity of his friend, found it still too commercial and disapproved of Daudet's concern with the public's demand.[27] Like *Jack*, *Le Nabab* was successfully performed at the Vaudeville Theater in 1880.

In the summer of 1878, Julia gave birth to a son whom the Daudets named Lucien. On the whole, the family was happy but the relationship between Daudet, satisfied with the bourgeois republic, and his brother Ernest, who had remained a staunch legitimist, took a turn for the worse. Daudet was also plagued by rheumatism in his right arm and writing became painful. After months of research he finished another political novel. *Les Rois en exil* (1879) is inspired by the fall of the kingdom of Illiria and tells the story of the exile of the royal family in Paris. There, comfortably installed, the old king awaits the end of political turmoil in his country and diverts himself with his mistresses until the new situation became hopeless and he realized that he would no longer be able to return to his country. Daudet's novel undoubtedly betrays his own disillusions concerning the French monarchy and the return of the Count of Chambord, living in Austria, but it also illustrates the importance that exile began to play as a theme in Daudet's imagination. Both the public and critics praised the book but its adaptation to the theater in 1883 was a failure and performances stopped after three weeks. This was the year when the Count of Chambord passed away with no descendants, thereby putting an end to the French branch of the Bourbon dynasty.

The year 1880 was marked by a sad event for Daudet and his friends. On March 20, Daudet accompanied by Zola, Goncourt, Maupassant and publisher Charpentier, had paid a visit to Flaubert in Croisset. The group enjoyed another great weekend boating on the Seine, dining on turbot and drinking fine wines, but a couple of weeks later, on May 8, Flaubert died following an epileptic seizure. The death of such a literary figure was a heavy blow to the rest of the group. The funeral took place in Rouen and was attended by a large crowd headed by Daudet and Goncourt. With the death of his beloved mentor and with age slowly weighing heavier every year, Daudet found himself constantly dreaming about Provence and, in a small green notebook, he began writing information concerning its climate, proverbs, social customs, and songs. He also recorded the characteristics of the language and culture and was particularly fascinated with the differences in temperament between North and South. His idea was to write a series of

biographies of famous Provençals such as Mirabeau and the Marquis de Sade but he never accomplished such projects and wrote instead another novel, *Numa Roumestan* (1881), which he originally entitled "Nord et Sud."

Numa Roumestan is another exile, who, at the age of twenty-two, left his native Provence to pursue his law studies in Paris. Like Daudet himself, Roumestan is inevitably trapped by the capital and, except for occasional visits, never returned home. After successfully passing his bar examinations, Roumestan marries Rosalie, a beautiful young woman, daughter of a prominent Northern man and Provençal mother. Unfortunately for Roumestan, Rosalie takes after her father and hates the South, unlike her sister Hortense. Roumestan is not a faithful husband and one day Rosalie, pregnant, catches him in the act with his mistress. Deeply upset by the incident, she miscarries. The portrait that Daudet gives us of Roumestan reminds us of Jansoulet in *Le Nabab* and is not complimentary. But Daudet is a realist and represents nature the way he sees it. Roumestan is proud and animated by a powerful sensuality which he cannot restrain and, like Jansoulet, takes a liking to politics. During one of his occasional visits to Provence, Numa is moved by the performance of Valmajour, a local *Tambourinaire* or tambourine and fife player, and invites him to Paris promising him a career in music. Valmajour takes Roumestan's invitation seriously, sells his house and, anxious to embark on a new career, leaves with his family for Paris. Embarrassed, Roumestan feels obligated and helps the poor man perform in front of Parisian audiences but to no avail, and his talent fails to arouse the interest of the public. In the meantime, Rosalie, having discovered her husband's recent affair with a young Provençal opera singer, threatens to divorce him. But after a conversation with her parents she forgives her husband once more. However, disillusioned with love and men she turns her affection to her children.

Numa Roumestan was Daudet's favorite novel, not so much because of its shrewd analysis of a politician's life, but because he enjoyed writing about the differences between Northern and Southern cultures. The North, represented by Rosalie and her father, is described as cold, serious and industrious, whereas Provence with Roumestan, Bompard, Hortense and her mother, is portrayed as lively, happy, sensual and passionate. In Daudet's understanding, the gap between North and South was too wide and communication almost impossible. When Mrs. Valmajour arrives in Paris she feels as much of a foreigner as a Swede or a Russian.[28] Daudet never hid his cultural preferences but in his book

he made an effort to give a balanced view of North and South. Unlike his wife who is an educated woman with refined taste and sensitive to the arts, Roumestan is lazy, exuberant and impulsive. His manners are that of a boor. He loves good wine and gourmet dinners, never refuses a cigar, and dresses slovenly. He can be eloquent but very often boisterous and constantly exaggerates or worse, lies. Finally Roumestan is not a faithful husband and believes that women should confine themselves to their motherly duties and be good wives. He is the epitome of male chauvinism and always prefers the company of his male friends whom he often invites to his house without having consulted his wife.

Critics applauded its adaptation to theater in 1887. Henry James called the novel "a masterpiece...a perfect work."[29] According to him, Daudet had truly surpassed himself and his novel showed "no weakness, no roughness" and presented "a compact and harmonious whole."[30] Daudet had been a favorite of James's for some time already. The two had met for the first time at Flaubert's in January 1876 when Turgenev introduced him to the cenacle and they saw each other again during one of his stays in Paris in February 1885, at the Daudets. James had a profound admiration for Daudet and his friends, although, like many, he felt a little uncomfortable with Zola's naturalism. In a letter to his friend Howells, he wrote:

> There is nothing more interesting to me now than the effort and experiment of this little group, with its truly infernal intelligence of art, from and manner—its intense artistic life. They do the only kind of work, today, that I respect.[31]

Daudet was especially dear to him because his prose exuded an uncommon and irresistible charm. "He cannot put three words together" James remarked, "that I don't more or less adore them."[32] According to him, Daudet was undoubtedly modern but, unlike other writers of the realist school, he alone had an "inveterate poetical touch,"[33] and a "light, quick, joyous, yet reflective, imagination," qualities which he readily attributed to his Southern temperament.[34] James met Daudet again in 1889, 1893 and 1995.

Each year Daudet's health grew worse and he began treatment for his rheumatism at Néris-les-Bains, near Vichy. He then traveled with his family to Grindelwald and Gersau in Switzerland. In the fall of 1882, shortly after his mother's funeral, *Le Figaro* began the serial publication of his latest Parisian novel, *L'Evangéliste* which came out as a

book in 1883. Like most of Daudet's stories, the topic was based on a true story, one that this time happened to his son Léon's German teacher. *L'Evangéliste* relates how Eline Ebsen, a twenty-year-old Danish woman falls prey to the teaching of Jeanne Autheman, a Protestant religious fanatic and wife of a successful banker. Literally bewitched, Eline abandons her widowed mother and joins Autheman's sect. After training, she is sent on missions throughout Europe. Her mother does her best to bring her daughter back, but government officials and lawyers refuse to fight the powerful banker. Only Reverend Aussandon is bold enough to accuse Jeanne Autheman in his sermons at church but his public denunciation is in vain. One day Eline finally reappears at her mother's house but years of mystical practices and drug consumption, against her will, have totally ruined her health and her condition is hopeless. Soon Eline leaves again and this time for good. Dedicated to Dr. Jean Charcot, the famous neurologist, the story met with success and critics appreciated "the literary and artistic qualities of the book, its terse and yet harmonious language, its light, free, natural style and the simplicity of its well-knit plot."[35]

By 1883, Daudet was a well-established novelist and literary figure. He was mentioned in Anatole France's study *Les Romanciers Contemporains* and a German scholar had written a two-volume study of his work.[36] The French Academy began to seek his candidature to replace a seat left vacant by the death of Jules Sandeau, George Sand's former lover. Zola and Goncourt urged Daudet to consider this opportunity but, like Mistral, Daudet hated all formal clubs and associations, and politely declined the offer. Incidentally, rumors about his possible candidacy brought him the animosity of Albert Delpit, another candidate for the seat who wrote an injurious article on Daudet. Insulted, Daudet challenged him to a duel and wounded his opponent in the arm. The case was closed. Dinners with his friends were not what they used to be. Turgenev died in 1883. Daudet's health did not improve despite his stays at Néris-les-Bains. Only the occasional trips to Provence seemed to work. There in the dry heat and in the merry company of Mistral, Daudet recovered his spirits and felt better.

Provence was again on Daudet's mind when he wrote his next novel. First serialized in the *Echo de Paris* (1884), *Sapho,* inspired by his affair with Marie Rieu, describes the love between Jean Gaussin, son of a rich Southern family, who works for the government in Paris and Fanny Legrand, an artist's model, also known as Sapho. Minor characters, such as Jean's uncle Césaire, incapable of good work and given

to gambling, or Déchelette, the unhappy painter, poet La Gournerie, and sculptor Caoudal, are more successfully portrayed than similar characters of his preceding novels. *Sapho* is above all the beautiful love story of Jean and Fanny. After living together for five years, Jean finally yields to Sapho's desire to adopt a child. But as time passes and Sapho's maternal instinct develops, Jean's love dwindles and he finally succumbs to the charms of another woman, Irène. However, before long, Jean goes back to Sapho but discovers that the child she has adopted is, in fact, the fruit of a former love affair. But his love for Sapho is so strong that he definitively cancels his wedding plans with Irène. Jean and Sapho plan to travel together. He leaves for Marseilles and patiently awaits Sapho who finally informs him that she will not come. *Sapho* was a consecration and Goncourt clearly saw that it was Daudet's best novel.[37] The play, which premiered on December 18, 1885, was a triumph.

At the beginning of 1885, the Daudets moved again to their new quarters in 31 Rue Bellechasse, in rich Saint-Germain. The house had been the former residence of Mme de Genlis and was surrounded with gardens planted with acacias and elm trees. Daudet quickly recreated his favorite Provençal atmosphere.[38] In his writing room on the second floor was his library with his favorite writers Virgil, Montaigne, Mistral and Aubanel. The Charcots lived next door on Boulevard St Germain and were frequent guests at their Thursday dinners attended now by a new vanguard composed of Stephane Mallarmé, Anatole France, and Pierre Loti. The summer months were usually spent in Champrosay, where Daudet, when not at his desk, would play chess with his mother-in-law or *boules* with his brother and son. Unfortunately, with age his physical condition worsened. The treatment recommended by Dr. Potain seemed to have little effect. In fact, he was constantly in pain and occasionally suffered from bouts of paralysis. Several times a day his son gave him morphine injections, which provided but temporary relief. Finally, one day, his doctor discovered that the cause of all his torment was in fact syphilis and immediately sent him over to Charcot. The latter confirmed his colleague's diagnostic and prescribed spas in Switzerland and Lamalou-les-Bains, near Montpellier. This helped little but provided Daudet with the rest he needed. He now knew that his days were numbered. The dreadful disease had claimed the lives of Baudelaire and Jules Goncourt, and Maupassant was also terminally ill. Walking became painful and Daudet had to use a stick. His body, Goncourt remarked, was often shaking and writhing like an earthworm. Still, Daudet carried on writing, attended dinners at his friends' homes, and,

whenever he felt better, he and Goncourt would take a train bound for the South.

Julia herself was very busy at home with their newborn Edmée but she continued to assist her husband with his novels, and even managed to do some writing of her own. In 1887, Chavaray published her *L'Enfance d'une Parisienne* and two years later *Enfants et Mères*. Shortly after the birth of their third child, the Daudets decided that the family house of Champrosay was too crowded and so acquired one of their own where they could entertain their numerous guests without imposing on the Allarts. Daudet's brother Ernest was now editor of *Le Petit Moniteur* and continued to pour forth biographies and novels. It was in Champrosay, in the small upstairs room, that Daudet wrote his next story *Tartarin sur les Alpes* (1885), a sequel to the adventures of the illustrious Provençal hunter now at work in the Swiss Alps. Tartarin hunts deer but also gets involved with politics when he meets Russian nihilists and his actions become suspicious to the local police. These new adventures are not as entertaining as the first ones and the book suffers from a lack of unity, although the same elements (caricatures, situation comedy) are present. However, due to the fame of its author the book sold well.

Daudet, now severely handicapped by his health problems, never lost his jovial character and often times, when at Goncourt's, he entertained and amused the guests.[39] In May 1885, *L'Arlésienne* was performed again at the Odéon theater and this time met with unequaled success. In September, after his treatment at Lamalou, the Daudets went to Provence and stayed with the Parrocels in Orgon, south of Avignon. With Goncourt, who had been coaxed into joining them for three weeks, they visited Mistral and Aubanel, toured the country (Les Baux, Avignon, Saint-Rémy), attended local dances and feasted on anchovies, pizzas, garlic, onions, tasted watermelons and local wines. Daudet had not felt better in a long time and returned to Paris eager to start a new story.

His novel *L'Immortel* (1888) tells the story of Léonard Astier-Réhu, a history scholar whose lifelong dream of becoming the Director of the French Academy finally comes true. Astier's wife, who does not share her husband's passion for history, sells some of his manuscripts to help their son Paul out of financial difficulty. Paul, like his mother, does not understand his father's research and spends his days courting rich widows. In the meantime, the experts closely examine the manuscripts and discover that they have been forged. Informed, Astier checks his sources and realizes he has been fooled and, unable to face shame and ridicule, drowns himself in the Seine. In this story Daudet gave a very critical

view of literary fame and of the inner workings of the French institution, revealing its intrigues, secret love affairs, and briberies. Astier owed his appointment to his wife, herself the daughter of a former member of the Academy.

In 1890, Daudet's eldest son Léon married Jeanne Hugo, granddaughter of the poet and the year after, became the proud father of a son, Charles. Léon soon abandoned his medical studies to take an active part in politics and, following in his parents' footsteps, started writing fiction. The same year, Daudet's third Tartarin book, *Port-Tarascon* was published. This was the first time however, that Tartarin's adventures were triggered by a historical fact. Between 1879 and 1881, several thousands of Bretons had emigrated to the new colony of Port Breton, on a Pacific island, only to find out that they had been tricked and that the plots of land that Du Breil de Brays had sold them did not exist. A trial ensued and Du Breil was sentenced to four years in jail. Daudet's imagination saw in this story a good topic for Tartarin and he set to work. In Daudet's version, Port Breton becomes Port-Tarascon and the Bretons are replaced by the Provençals. The Duke of Mons is the impostor who supposedly bought an island from a Papua when, in truth, it belonged to the British government. The latter soon discovers the hoax and eventually repatriates all the victims to Provence. Tartarin who had emigrated with the others was mistakenly held responsible for the disaster and sent to jail. Fortunately, he was later acquitted but his reputation had suffered and moved across the Rhône in Beaucaire where he died shortly after. James translated the novel into English.[40]

Daudet could only travel with difficulty and trips to Provence were not recommended. However, Provençals came to see him, including a young poet by the name of Batisto Bonnet. The two men often met and spent long hours conversing in Provençal. Daudet enjoyed Bonnet's poems and translated them into French. He continued to have an active interest in Provence and in 1891 he wrote a letter in Provençal to encourage and congratulate the new Marseillais review *La Sartan.* In 1893, Daudet finally accepted to become member of Academy of his native city of Nîmes, and even agreed to chair in the yearly meeting of the Société des Félibres de Paris. However, around that time and for obscure reasons, Arène and Daudet had stopped seeing each other. In 1895, Daudet's health seemed to improve and he seized the opportunity to travel with his family. They first went to Italy and then to England where they were James's guests. Together, the old friends visited Westminster Abbey, Oxford and Windsor, and James introduced Daudet to Edmund

Gosse and George Meredith who, at Flint Cottage, read aloud excerpts from Mistral's *Poème du Rhône*. Late in June the Daudets went home, delighted with their stay on the other side of the Channel.

In December 1896, Daudet learned of Arène's death who passed away in Antibes where he was resting. He was only fifty-four years old. A few months later Goncourt died in Daudet's arms at Champrosay. Daudet was heart broken. Meanwhile *Sapho* triumphed at the Odéon Theater. Daudet spent the last months of his life bedridden and in pain. He passed away on December 16, 1897and was buried in Père Lachaise, near his parents, after a ceremony attended by numerous celebrities including Zola who read the eulogy. Mistral, fearing the damp weather might worsen his cold had remained at home. Julia continued to live in Paris, attended women's meetings, and edited her husband's correspondence and posthumous works. She also traveled to Tourraine to her parents' new estate and wrote poetry and her memoirs. She died in 1940 at the age of ninety-six. Léon passed away in 1942. Lucien wrote the first biography of his friend Empress Eugénie and died in 1947.

Unlike Zola, Daudet's life long exile in the capital enhanced his attachment to his native land. Balzac, Flaubert and Goncourt certainly influenced his art but, as James correctly observed, Daudet always managed to insert a distinctive poetic touch, too often absent in the more rigorous art of his masters. As he explains in his *Souvenirs d'un Homme de Lettres,* his portraits are mosaic compositions. Towns, scenery and places, are not represented as they really are, but rather composed from various images.

The town of Apt in *Numa Roumestan,* for instance, is actually the composite drawing of Nîmes and Aix-en-Provence. Daudet proceeded in the same manner for his characters and thereby anticipated the art of Giono. Joseph Conrad loved the dramatic element of his stories: "Daudet did not whisper; he spoke loudly, with animation, with a clear felicity of tone as a bird sings. He saw life around him with extreme clearness, and he felt it as it is thinner than air and more elusive than a flash of lightning."[41] Conrad, however, failed to see the poetic and humorous side of Daudet, that which linked him to Mistral and other Provençal storytellers. "Yes I am a Southerner, I truly am. All my childhood sensitivity, all my inspiration comes from the South."[42] His exile had taught him that that Provence was inescapable. "Terrible Midi! Pas moyen de lui échapper..." declares Roumestan.[43] But Daudet's art also reflects the difficult compromise that an ambitious Provençal author like himself had to face, namely to appeal to the Parisian audience and critics

without renouncing the culture which fashioned his sensitivity: "Prenons garde au Midi…. N'en abusons pas…. Paris se fatiguerait."[44]

Endnotes

1. Jacques-Henry Bornecque, *Les Années d'Apprentissage d'Alphonse Daudet* (Paris: Nizet, 1951) 42.

2. Alain Gérard, *Le Midi de Daudet* (Aix-en-Provence: Edisud, 1988) 20.

3. Alphonse Daudet, *Le Petit Chose* (Paris: Livre de Poche, 1984) 22.

4. Jacques Rouré, *Alphonse Daudet* (Paris: Julliard, 1982) 19.

5. Daudet, *Le Petit Chose* 54.

6. Bornecque, *Les Années d'Apprentissage d'Alphonse Daudet* 171–72.

7. "A mesure que Mistral parlait, une bonne odeur, fraîche et vivace, de mon pays depuis longtemps quitté, remplissait l'étroite chambre. Je le retrouvais dans un coin de Paris, ce délicieux parfum de Provence, en écoutant cette belle langue, sonore et musicale…" Marie-Thérèse Jouveau, *Alphonse Daudet, Maître des Tendresses* (Aix-en-Provence: Jouveau, 1990) 55–56.

8. "Le logis du poète est à l'extrémité du pays; c'est la dernière maison à gauche, sur la route de Saint-Rémy, une maisonnette à étage avec un jardin devant." Daudet, *Lettres de mon Moulin* (Paris: Presses Pocket, 1990) 126.

9. Bornecque, *Histoire d'une Amitié: Correspondance Inédite entre Alphonse Daudet et Frédéric Mistral 1860 1897* (Paris: Julliard, 1979) 122–23.

10. Daudet, *Lettres de mon Moulin* 210.

11. "Souple et leste dans sa petite taille…sa barbe molle en pointe,…son teint mat mais chaud…Paul Arène avait une grâce paysanne et charmante qui faisait songer à celle d'un joli chevrier grec." Léopold Dauphin, *Paul Arène* (Béziers: Société de Musicologie du Languedoc, 1912) 14.

12. Daudet, *Lettres de mon Moulin* 210.

13. Daudet 18.

14. Henri James, *Partial Portrait* (London: Macmillan, 1888) 195.

15. Daudet, *Lettres de mon Moulin* 47.

16. "Un foulatoun, un fantasi que fai dinda e trelusi tout ça que toco." Bornecque, *Histoire d'une Amitié* 167.

17. Murray Sachs, *The Career of Alphonse Daudet: A Critical Study* (Cambridge: Harvard UP, 1965) 70–71.

18. "C'est purement et simplement un *chef-d'oeuvre*. Je lâche le mot et je le maintiens. Tout, absolument tout, m'a diverti, plusieurs fois j'ai ri tout haut aux éclats." Gustave Flaubert, *Correspondance* 3 vols (Paris: Librairie de France, 1928–29) III: 60.

19. "C'est la guerre, assure-t-il, qui l'a transformé, qui a éveillé au fond de lui l''dée qu'il pouvait mourir sans avoir rien fait, sans rien laisser de durable…. Alors seulement il s'est mis au travail, et avec le travail est née chez lui l'ambition littéraire." Edmond and Jules de Goncourt, *Journal,* 3 vols. (Paris: Laffont, 1989) II: 1127.

20. "Ça vous fera rire. C'est très gentil. Il y a là-dedans une veine comique

réelle." *Gustave Flaubert-George Sand: Correspondance* (Paris: Flammarion, 1981) 380.

21. Flaubert's *Le Candidat,* Daudet's *L'Arlésienne,* Goncourt's *Henriette Maréchal* and *La Patrie en Danger,* as well as Zola's *Thérèse Raquin* and *Les Héritiers Rabourdin* had failed.

22. *Gustave Flaubert–George Sand: Correspondance* 485.

23. "J'ai rarement lu une oeuvre à la fois plus exquise et plus poignante." Emile Zola, *Correspondance,* 9 vols. (Montréal: Presses de l'Université, 1978–1993) II: 374, note 4.

24. "*Jack* contient les plus beaux morceaux que vous ayez encore écrits." Zola, *Correspondance* II: 440.

25. "Je suis content que *Jack* vous ait plu. C'est un charmant livre, n'est-ce pas? Si vous connaissiez l'auteur vous l'aimeriez encore plus que son oeuvre." *Gustave Flaubert–George Sand: Correspondance* 530.

26. *Correspondance* 531.

27. "Trop de condescendance pour les goûts littéraires du gros public." Goncourt, *Journal* II: 755.

28. "...aussi égarée, aussi étrangère, dans la capitale de la France, que si elle fût arrivée de Stockholm ou de Nijni-Novgorod." Daudet, *Numa Roumestan* (Paris: Librairie de France, 1929) 70.

29. James, *Partial Portraits* 197.

30. James 197.

31. Leon Edel, *Henry James: A Life* (New York: Harper & Row, 1985) 300.

32. Edel 440.

33. Edel 207.

34. Edel 205.

35. Alphonse Roche, *Alphonse Daudet* (Boston: Twayne Publishers, 1976) 73.

36. Adolf Gerstmann, *Alphonse Daudet, sein Leben und seine Werke bis zum Jahre 1883,* 2 vols. (Berlin: Auerbach, 1883).

37. "Le livre le plus complet, le plus *humain* qu'il ait fait. Son talent jusqu'alors un peu féminin, devient dans ce roman un talent de mâle." Goncourt, *Journal* II:1078.

38. " Le pétrin, la huche, la pannetière; le tout en vieux chêne ouvré, vous transportent subitement dans un intérieur provençal des plus authentiques," remarked guest Jules Hoche. Cited in Marie-Thérèse Jouveau, *Alphonse Daudet, Maître des Tendresses* 175.

39. "Daudet est le boute-en-train, l'amuseur, le causeur *commediante,* le bruit, le mouvement, l'esprit bouffon des dimanches du *Grenier.*" Goncourt, *Journal* III: 34.

40. Published by Little & Brown, 1890.

41. Joseph Conrad, *Notes on Life and Letters* (Freeport New York, 1972) 23.

42. "J'en suis du Midi, j'en suis bien. Toute ma sensibilité d'enfant, ma source naturelle vient de là." Cited in Jean-Paul Clebert, *Les Daudet* (Paris: Presses de la Renaissance, 1988) 283.

43. Daudet, *Numa Roumestan* 81.

44. Daudet 144.

Four

Henri Bosco

At a time when Daudet, Mistral and the *Félibres* were receiving international recognition, Provence gave birth to another child who was to become one of its most devoted poets. "Je suis né à Avignon, rue de La Carreterie, au numéro 3," wrote Henri Bosco in his memoirs.[1] He was born on November 16, 1888 in the market district of Avignon where saddlers, grocers, wine sellers and bakers worked side by side in the narrow cobbled streets. The place was animated, picturesque and friendly, and Bosco never forgot its distinctive aroma of leather mixed with coffee, wheat, wool and sulfur. The people who lived in this part of the city spoke mainly Provençal and Bosco's family was no exception. Ties with Avignon were only recent in Bosco's ancestry, for his paternal grandfather, Jacques, was native of Piedmont but had left for Marseilles to work in a soap factory. Jacques married and had three sons, Thomas, Baptistin, Louis (Bosco's father), and a daughter, Philomène. All grew up in Marseilles's *Vieux Quartiers,* perched on a

63

Henri Bosco 1888–1976 (Photograph Fond Bosco, University of Nice).

hill guarded at the top by Notre Dame des Accoules. The view over the bay is beautiful. By trade, Bosco's father was an opera singer (tenor). He married Louise Faléna from Nice and the couple later settled in Avignon. Louise had difficult pregnancies and lost four babies.[2] Henri was their fifth and last child. Mr. Bosco was a hardworking man but in his spare time he loved telling stories often accompanying himself with a guitar that he had built by hand. As a child, Bosco loved to listen to his father's tales of Provençal shepherds that he usually invented on the spot. Mr. Bosco had indeed "the soul of a troubadour" and his stories had a profound effect on the development of his son's artistic nature.[3]

The Boscos took great care of their young child, and even hired a nurse, Julie Jouve, to help them out. They wanted to make sure Henri grew strong and healthy. Mrs. Bosco herself was a loving mother but, unlike her husband, she was loquacious and temperamental. She was

also very religious and superstitious, and strongly believed in the existence of another world, particularly in ghosts. "She had a vivid and powerful imagination and from the most ordinary object she would concoct most uncommon forms," Bosco remembers.[4] More than anything else, Mrs. Bosco feared spells and curses. As a young man, Henri was essentially a dreamer, fascinated by the presence of the supernatural and its many but subtle manifestations on earth. As an artist, later in life, he walked the thin borders between consciousness and dreams. "Everyone knows," he once remarked in a characteristic manner, "that dreams force the mind to benevolence. To think is to bite. To dream is to caress simple images."[5]

When he turned three, his family moved south to the country on the road to Châteaurenard. "Thus I grew up with the scents of the earth, of wheat and new wine," Bosco recalls in *Antonin*.[6] The *Mas du Gage*, as the place was called, was a large two-story farmhouse with a yard surrounded by a small stone wall covered with moss that smelled like honey. His room was upstairs and had a view of large fields lined with cypress-trees, planted as a protection from the cold *mistral*. Farther out the road slowly meandered through tall poplars and gentle weeping willows. It was there, amongst orchards and vineyards, that Bosco lived until the age of seventeen. Years of residence in Italy and North Africa in his adult life did not tarnish his love of Provence and the memory of his youth in Avignon and the Lubéron remained his major source of inspiration. "It is everything to me. It is an addiction. I have loved it all my life," he wrote in his memoirs.[7]

Being, like Jean Giono, an only child, life on the *mas* had its lonely moments for Bosco but his nurse Julie, a native of Bédoin at the foot of Mount Ventoux, was there to entertain him with her good spirit and local legends. Storytelling was a favorite pastime around the house. When it was not his father or Julie, it was a local shepherd, who told tales of the mysterious Lubéron mountains. "These stories had a profound effect on me and I dreamed of them throughout my childhood," Bosco says in *L'Habitant de Sivergues*.[8] Bosco learned how to read on the farm by perusing magazines with articles on famous French buccaneers such as Surcouf, Jean Bart, and Suffren. At the time his favorite author was Alexandre Dumas. "When I was alone with Mother while her *daube* was simmering, we would reminisce about the perilous adventures of d'Artagnan, Ann of Austria and the evil Cardinal Richelieu. The kitchen was literally transformed."[9] But Dumas had other fierce competitors such as Fenimore Cooper or Balzac, and *The Spy* as well as

Les Chouans captivated his young imagination. Life on the *mas* was occasionally interrupted by family outings to Marseilles where his cousins still lived. These trips delighted young Bosco who loved the bustling activity, clear horizons, and bright colors of Marseilles. Its *Vieux Quartiers,* a veritable medieval labyrinth of narrow cobbled streets and shops, were certainly a safe playground, but it was the old harbor, later immortalized by Pagnol, that fascinated Bosco. There he mingled with fishermen wearing their colorful costumes, observed sailors from Corfu, Majorca or Sicily play cards at café terraces, and wandered about ships from the West Indies or Africa, intoxicated by the mixtures of aromas of saffron, pepper, coffee, rum, bananas and oranges.

Marseilles and the sea undoubtedly had an impact on the shaping of young Bosco's imagination but he remained above all a man of the hills. It was not the immediate landscape around the family *mas* or Avignon, which inspired him, for as he says in *Antonin*, "it was too flat,"[10] but rather the mysterious Lubéron mountain some twenty miles east. When he discovered the Lubéron, Bosco immediately succumbed to its charm. There lay hidden, almost imperceptible to the naked eye, forlorn isolated villages whose walls and stones reminded the visitor of the mysterious Templars and the Huguenot refugees. Bosco fell in love with the Lubéron and from then on called himself "a man of the hills."[11] But this is only partially true for Bosco's attachment to his beloved Lubéron is often disputed by the marshes of Vaccarès and the banks of the Durance.

Until the age of ten, Bosco was educated at home by his mother. Then his parents sent him to the Ortolans school in Avignon and later to the *lycée.* Bosco was a good student particularly in literature and the classics but he disliked being a boarder and missed his family and home too much. Unlike Mistral, he did not have the chance to meet a Roumanille with whom he could share his literary interests. To him, used to roaming about the countryside freely for years, school remained a jail and his days were filled with gloom and despair. He did however find some solace in books, Theocritus, Homer and especially Virgil, "the poet to whom, in all due proportion, I resemble the most."[12] But Bosco also attended the Music Conservatory after school where he studied the violin since his parents wanted him to become an orchestra conductor.

It was at school that Bosco discovered Mistral.[13] The poet's home was only a couple of miles away, and from his bedroom Bosco could see the church of the village. "For years I had before my eyes the entire

country sung about in *Mireio.* As an adolescent I walked in the country everywhere and at each step I would find the poet. When I come back here I find him again. He left an indelible mark on the area."[14] Bosco's classics professor revered the *Félibres* and would often take his class to the fields near Maillane where, sitting underneath an olive tree, he would read aloud entire passages from Mistral's book. Bosco admired Mistral's poetic genius and his struggle to preserve Provençal. His enthusiasm was so great that one day he paid the old poet a visit at his home. "I immediately took a liking to him. His presence was commanding yet familiar. He was often described as imperial and aloof but I never saw him like that. He had majesty, but his warm reception made his majesty human. One could love him."[15] Mistral made a profound impression on Bosco. In his opinion, the old poet was the epitome of wisdom. He was not only "the most important man," but above all "the absolute man," who, besides an "uncommon perfection," succeeded in blending into one harmonious whole "life, poetry, and wisdom."[16] Bosco was especially fascinated with the aura of serenity and mystery that surrounded the Provençal poet.

In 1907, Bosco was admitted to his *baccalauréat* exams and enrolled at the University of Grenoble where he majored in Italian. Little is known of his days there but he must have done well for he obtained his *licence* in 1909. He then lived in Florence for two years and returned to France to teach in Avignon. In 1912, he passed the *agrégation,* a competitive examination which certified him as a secondary school teacher, and began a long career which took him to Bourg-en-Bresse in lower Burgundy and then to Philippeville in Algeria, where he switched to French and the Classics. When World War I broke out, Bosco was drafted in the *Zouaves* regiment and fought in Greece, Albania, Egypt and Hungary. In 1919, he resumed civilian life and taught for one year in Belgrade and, in 1920, was appointed *Maître de Conférences* at the University of Grenoble and sent to the *Institut Français,* in Naples, where he stayed for ten years. There he visited Pompeii, studied Roman religion, perfected his knowledge of Dante, and met French writer Max Jacob and philosopher Jean Grenier. It was there, at the foot of Mount Vesuvio, in such a rich cultural and literary atmosphere that Bosco began to write. He had always loved writing and in school he had composed verse, but this time he was determined to be more serious about it. He had not forgotten his Provence where he returned in the summer months and especially the village of Lourmarin in the Lubéron where a friend of his, Robert Vibert, a businessman from Lyons, had bought

an old castle. Bosco discovered the place in 1922 and returned almost every summer thereafter, participating in its restoration.

Bosco's first novels were influenced by surrealism and particularly by Max Jacob and Jean Cocteau but Provence is also immediately present. His first novel *Pierre Lampédouze* (1924) tells the story of an aspiring young Parisian poet Pierre Lampédouze who, having recently inherited a small property in the Provençal village of Cucuron, decides to leave the City of Lights. Over the months, Pierre succumbs to the charm of Provence and when, after a visit to the *notaire* Pierre stumbles upon a copy of *Mireio,* his life is transformed. Bosco's novel was his first attempt at prose and contained some technical problems, especially in the plot structure, but Lampédouze's return to Provence symbolizes Bosco's own decision to sever himself from avant-garde literature and to turn to Provence for inspiration. With the surrealists however, Bosco shared a fascination for dreams. "I was born in dreams and for dreams I live," declares Joachim, the protagonist of *L'Epervier.*[17]

In his second novel *Irénée* (1929), Bosco shows the same Lampédouze in Naples this time and precisely on the island of Capri where he meets and falls in love with young Irénée. The story already emphasizes reverie and dreams that become, in fact, the very texture of the plot. Provence is present but still in the background. It is only with his next novel *Le Quartier de Sagesse* (1929) that Bosco finally sets his story in Provence. It is a tale of an unhappy (and complex) love story, between Captain Roger Maulieu and Suzanne, in which several other characters such as Roger's aunt, Mme Marlotte and her friends take part. The plot, somewhat reminiscent of Marivaux's theater as far as the quid pro quos are concerned, shows other characteristics of Bosco's style, namely a very slow development, and careful analysis of emotions, dreams and visions. Provence however, plays only a limited role and is reduced to the linguistic regionalisms of Ambroise, the fifty-year old waiter of the *Café des Négociants,* who uses words such as *espincher* (to spy), *escagasser* (clobber), *peuchère* (poor one, pity), *tafanari* (buttocks), *zou* (come on), *te* (here), and *ve* (look). The story is told in the traditional third person, a technique Bosco later abandoned.

In 1930, Bosco's stay in Italy came to an end and he returned to France where he married Madeleine Rhodes, daughter of a school principal from"uch in the Southwest. The Boscos then left for Bourg-en-Bresse, where he taught for a year. Bosco had not given up his literary ambitions and as soon as he had some time off, he wrote poems for *Le Feu* edited in Aix by Joseph d'Arbaud. The following year, the Boscos

left France for Morocco (Rabat) where he accepted a teaching position in the Lycée Gouraud. Fascinated by the desert and never far from his beloved Mediterranean, the Boscos remained in Morocco for the next twenty-four years. Bosco enjoyed teaching French literature and the classics and studied eastern mysticism and particularly Sufism. During the long stay there, he met with the numerous French expatriates, chaired *L'Alliance Française* and attended many literary soirées and garden parties. Every so often Bosco contributed articles to reviews such as *Les Cahiers du Sud, L'Arche*, or Les *Nouvelles Littéraires*.

But novels were what he enjoyed writing most. With *Le Sanglier* (1932), Bosco began a series of novels which take place in his favorite place, the Lubéron, which soon became a place of inspiration. It is there that René, the protagonist, spends his summer months in a rental property. To keep himself company, René hires the services of Marie Claire, a young orphan girl who prepares his meals and helps him around the house. The village is surrounded by an aura of mystery and René's curious nature forces him to investigate some of the inhabitants' strange behaviors. During a wild boar hunt in which René participates, Marie is killed. Bosco's novel centers on the mysterious and powerful wild boar, and inevitably brings to mind d'Arbaud's tale *La Bèstio dou Vacarés* (1926).

D'Arbaud, a long time friend, was a major influence in Bosco's early development. Born in 1874 in the small village of Meyrargues, a few miles north of Aix, he was raised in a family with strong traditions and where Provençal was the language spoken at home. His mother Marie was the daughter of Valère-Martin, a scholar and archeologist with a keen interest in Provence's past, and a friend of Mistral's. Encouraged by her father, Marie wrote poetry and collaborated on the *Armana*. Like Bosco, d'Arbaud went to school in Avignon where he befriended Mistral, Roumanille, Felix Gras, Clovis Hugues, Marius Jouveau and Folco de Baroncelli, a distant cousin. From 1893 to 1897, d'Arbaud studied law in Aix but continued to write poems, which he sent to Mistral, and frequented Provençal circles. In Aix, he met Joachim Gasquet and Valère Bernard, then *Majoral* of the *Félibres*. In 1897, d'Arbaud left Aix for the Camargue where his cousin de Baroncelli lived on a ranch. Fascinated by the beauty and wilderness of the place, d'Arbaud settled there and became a *manadier* or bull-raiser but he never abandoned literature and continued to write Provençal tales and poems, which he published in local magazines. In 1946, he married and moved back to Aix where his wife was a teacher. He died there in 1950.

Marie d'Arbaud 1834–1871 (Museon Arlaten, Arles photography Delgado).

D'Arbaud's *La Bèstio dou Vacarés* was published in Paris by Grasset in 1926 in Provençal, with a French translation. The story takes place in the 14th century and tells of the uncanny encounter between Jacques Roubaud, a *gardian* or bull herder, and a wild and proud creature, half goat, half man and endowed with language. Soon the protagonist and the beast become friends but over the months the creature, suffering from hunger and old age, shows signs of weakness and despair, and disappears forever while Roubaud goes home to fetch food for him. The novel was the opportunity for d'Arbaud to celebrate the Camargue, a desert of salty marshes, battered by high winds and inhabited by a few solitary men who raise bulls for traditional bullfights. Bosco held d'Arbaud in high esteem and considered him"the greatest Provençal poet since Mistral."[18] The two authors shared a love of solitude and wilderness and their writings are pervaded with spirits and myths. D'Arbaud's book had a long-lasting influence on Bosco who, in *Le Récif* (1971), dedicated to his friend, recalls: "I read the book slowly, solemnly, with passion from sunset to midnight almost without interruption."[19] Bosco saw in d'Arbaud's beast the last survivors of the ancient gods.

With *Le Sanglier* Bosco turned his inspiration to the Lubéron and the village of Lourmarin became a spiritual place, "un lieu où souffle l'esprit."[20] At this time Provence is constantly on his mind. In 1933 he gave a lecture on Mistral in Rabat. Although he wrote prose, Bosco liked to think of himself as a poet. "In my mind, without poetry, literature does not exist," he declared later in his life.[21] The novel as a well-defined genre did not interest him and, except in a few cases, he called

his stories "récits," "contes" or even "poèmes."[22] He admired poets more than novelists and amongst his favorites were Homer, Mistral, Dante and Petrarch. To some extent, the esoteric aspect of Bosco's tales also echoes the *trobar clus* technique of the troubadours. Realism, such as developed by Flaubert or Zola did not interest him. On the other hand, he enjoyed immensely Henri Fournier's *Le Grand Meaulnes* and Joseph Conrad. Bosco, notes Jean-Pierre Cauvin, is "un contemplatif," and his tales attempt to represent not the real or visible but the mysterious and hidden aspects of life. Bosco compared his inspiration to a "state of hallucination,"

Joseph d'Arbaud 1834–1950 (Photograph Editions Grasset, Paris).

which he strove to impart to the reader through his stories.[23] He defined himself as "un esprit extrêmement religieux" who, like Plotinus, believed in the interrelatedness of things.[24] According to him, the planets, the earth, plants, animals, as well as humans, past and present, were all invariably linked and a manifestation of God, a characteristic that, incidentally, we also find in Giono's early novels.

Bosco, again, like Giono, was strongly attached to his native land. The *notaire* is an omnipresent character in his stories and symbolizes the importance of place and tradition. He is also responsible for the transmission of the tangible order of things between members of the same family and his function, like that of the priest, is sacred. In *Le Trestoulas* (1935), for instance, Bosco describes one of these ancestral feuds which traditionally opposed Provençal families. Clapu, a solitary farmer, refuses to sell, as he had promised to do, a plot of barren land called Trestoulas. The prospective buyers, the Matourets, a clan of rogues, are angered by this and determined to do everything in their

power to acquire this land. They use every trick and cunning in their power to force Clapu to change his mind but to no avail. Finally, they set fire to Clapu's farm. To avenge himself, the latter, who in the meantime has discovered the original spring in an underground cave which provides water for the village, blocks it. The consequences of his act are disastrous for the Matourets. Their crops fail, their cattle die and soon they are forced, like the rest of the villagers, to leave the place, an episode which may have been suggested by Giono's *Colline* (1929) and probably influenced, in turn, Pagnol's famous *Manon des Sources*. In *L'Habitant de Sivergues* (1935) also situated in the Lubéron country, Bosco, like Giono once again, summons back to life the rich cultural and spiritual past of the once-thriving village of Sivergues. The narrator, intrigued by the discovery of an old diary written by a country priest, explores the back country and, to his great surprise, discovers a forgotten resident, the last descendant of a group of Huguenots, who, a couple of centuries previously, sought refuge in this deserted mountain and founded the village.

Bosco's wife Madeleine was always supportive of his literary activities and he would often read her his stories and attentively listen to her comments. She encouraged him to write and, according to his own accounts, was influential in his choice of the Lubéron for the setting of his novels. They had no children of their own, but Bosco loved childhood and had kept fond memories of his youth. With *L'Âne Culotte* (1937), he began a series of children's tales that brought him recognition. It is probably Bosco's best story and one of the few books of his still in print. Like Alain Fournier, Bosco seemed to have been naturally attracted to childhood because it is a magical time, a world full of spirits and mysteries and where dreams acquire a reality of their own. "A child does not live, like us, in a (seemingly) logical world but in an imaginary environment...He does not face objects but lives right in the middle of them," Bosco thus shows the deep affinities with his own artistic mind.[25]

The tale takes place in a small Provençal village surrounded by orchards and vineyards and where the scent of burning firewood mixes with the aroma of freshly baked bread. This is the home of Constantin Gloriot, a young boy, and of Saturnin and Saturnine, his grandparents, Anselme the shepherd, Peguinotte, the maid and Hyacinthe, the waif. One day, Constantin, intrigued by the visit of a beautiful wild donkey to the neighborhood, follows him to his home in the domain of Belles-Tuiles, in the hill country. There, Constantin discovers an enchanted

garden where enormous vegetables grow and wild animals roam in peace. He makes the acquaintance of Cyprien, the secretive and solitary older fellow who created this small oasis. Constantin later learns from the village priest that Cyprien traveled around the world and actually lived on an island where perfect harmony reigned between men and animals. But the arrival of merchants upset the delicate social order of the happy islanders and finally put an end to their idyllic lives. Cyprien left the island and went to Provence to be near the priest who had once cured him of a strange disease.

Over the years, Cyprien recreated a happy oasis but the death of a beautiful fox killed by the *caraques* or gypsies, on their way to their yearly pilgrimage to the Saintes-Maries, disrupted that peace. In the end, Cyprien and Hyacinthe mysteriously disappear. Bosco wrote this tale in a traditional manner, using the third person and made use of dialogues, two factors that undoubtedly contributed to its success. The character of Hyacinthe reappears in two other books *Hyacinthe* (1940) and *Le Jardin d'Hyacinthe* (1946). The latter also introduces Méjan de Mégrémut, who lives alone in the barren hills with his maid, Sidonie, his shepherd Arnaviel who, in addition to a thorough knowledge of plant and animal life, can tell all the traditional tales and legends. Mégrémut, intrigued by the uncommon spiritual aura of the place, investigates the local legends and finds out that the village was built on an ancient gypsy place of worship.

Solitude is a major theme in Bosco's novels. "He belongs, like many others, to the race of silent Southerners," once declared Marseillais poet Louis Brauquier.[26] He was a solitary being himself and loved long walks in the Lubéron. Writing was for him an act of inspiration, which required silence and concentration. He could not, like Paul Arène for instance, write in crowded cafés. He did not plan his stories but let them develop naturally. In one of his best novels, *Le Mas Théotime* (1945), Bosco moved his plot to Cézanne's countryside at the foot of Mount Sainte-Victoire behind Aix-en-Provence. The story revolves around the relationship between two cousins and enemies Pascal Dérivat and Clodius. Clodius finally decides that the best way to get rid of his cousin is to buy his land and so makes Pascal an offer. But the latter naturally refuses, which angers Clodius and provokes him to set fire to his cousin's fields. While the battle between the two men rages on, Pascal falls in love with his cousin Geneviève who has come for a visit.

Tragedy begins when Clodius is found dead in his home, shot by two bullets. Shortly before the police arrive, Pascal discovers the

murderer hiding in his own home, with a slightly wounded ankle. The latter explains that, mistaking him for a burglar, Clodius had fired at him several times, and that he shot back only to defend himself, unfortunately killing him. Clearly the affair was an accident, and Pascal, feeling sympathy for the stranger, hides him from the police. But Pascal's help is only temporary and before long, the police manage to capture the stranger. Following the arrest, Pascal learns that the mysterious person was in fact Geneviève's husband from whom she had run away. Dumbfounded at the news of the incident, Geneviève seeks solace and refuge in a nearby convent. As Bosco himself admitted, his novel is one of the few in which he used a traditional technique of a plot and ending, which added to the action and sped up the usual slow pace of his stories. Critics and the public alike praised the book which was awarded the Renaudot Prize.

With the success as an author and after some thirty-five years as a teacher, Bosco finally decided to retire but he remained in Morocco another ten years. His mother Louise, who was living with him, died there in 1947, while he was working on his next story. *Monsieur Carre Benoît à la Campagne* (1947) continues along what became Bosco's favorite themes: a return to a land alive with spirits. Mr. Carre Benoît, a retired civil servant, and his wife Hermeline come to the small Provençal village of Aversols to take possession of a house they inherited from their aunt Hortense. But the transaction is not as simple as they thought and Ratou the *notaire* explains that the will prohibits the new owners from the attic, which must remain closed at all, times. It also requests that the new owners hire Zephyrine, the old maidservant. The Carre Benoîts are intrigued and soon begin to wonder what may lie behind the attic's door. Although retired, Mr. Carre Benoît has no intention of living like a recluse and he interests himself in the political life of the village. Soon his long administrative experience and keen sense of leadership enable him to be elected head of the post office and then mayor. However, and strangely enough, as he his is climbing up the social ladder again, his wife who up to that point was quiet and reserved, leaves her husband, and the novel ends.

Malicroix (1948) is another successful novel in which Bosco takes us to another mysterious part of Provence: the Camargue. It is there that young Martial Mégremut, whose family was first introduced in *Le Jardin d'Hyacinthe,* inherits a house with land from his great uncle and sailor Cornelius Malicroix. The latter had come there to rest in solitude after a life spent traveling around the world. It is in these deserted marshlands,

rich in wildlife and inhabited by a few grave and solitary men that Cornelius had decided to spend the rest of his days in the company of Balandran, the servant, and his dog. Martial does not adapt easily to his new solitary existence, for he himself comes from a family where sociability is the rule, but he finds it challenging. Cornelius's will specifically states, as Maître Dromiols the *notaire* reminds Martial, that to inherit the property, a minimum residency of three consecutive months is required. Intrigued by his uncle's will and fascinated with the wide deserted open lands, Martial soon finds himself at home in this strange environment. Over the months, this forlorn land, battered by warm gusty winds, and haunted by exotic birds, transforms Martial spiritually and he slowly becomes serene and at peace with himself. *Malicroix* contains some of Bosco's best descriptions of the hidden beauty of Provence and received the Prix des Ambassadeurs.

In his next novel *Sylvius* (1949) Bosco leaves aside his favorite themes of solitude and spiritual quest and focuses on village life and sociability. The Mégremuts, as we know, are ultimately social beings and their rich little town of Pontillargues with its sixteen hundred people, its judge and four or five *gendarmes* is the paragon of community life. Life there is so good and the inhabitants so happy that there is no record of anyone having ever left the place. Every night at dinnertime, one can see through the wide-open windows, smiling villagers diligently gathered around a tureen of soup and a loaf of bread. The Mégrémuts are a well-respected family, animated by a strict sense of kinship and a sincere reverence for their ancestors. They never fail to assemble to share their best moments as well as their sorrows and rarely venture outside of their town for, in their mind, an excursion to the neighboring village is a perilous undertaking that requires long preparations.

However, one day, sixty-year-old Sylvius, a family member who is a dreamer and plays the clarinet to his frogs, breaks the tradition and, on a cold winter morning, wanders away on his horse Melchior. After a few days of meandering through the country, Sylvius winds up in a mysterious valley where a company of traveling actors have temporarily set up camp. Sylvius befriends the artists, plays music with them and even participates in their plays. In the meantime, in Pontillargues, his family is worried about his absence and, with the assistance of local farmers, begins to search the area. The story ends when Sylvius is finally brought back home.

But Bosco soon returned to his favorite themes with another story *Le Rameau de la Nuit* (1950). The protagonist Frédéric Meyrel is a

young classical scholar who leaves Marseilles to live in a small village of Geneval in the Lubéron that he previously discovered during an outing. There he rents Loselee, a house whose owner Bernard mysteriously disappeared. Investigating the area, Frédéric makes the acquaintance of Valérie, Bernard's young deaf and mute servant, and Mus, his suspicious and secretive gardener. Later, Frédéric also meets Clothilde, Bernard's niece and former lover. Both the villagers and Clothide see in Frédéric an uncanny resemblance to Bernard and inform him. Intrigued, Frédéric begins to gather information on Bernard, on his past and on his mysterious disappearance, and in the process, he inevitably falls in love with Clothilde. Mus is outraged and out of dedication to his master, challenges Frédéric to a fight in which he is knocked unconscious. Fearing for his life, Frédéric leaves the village and later learns that Mus perished in a fire he set to the property. In spite of the definite suspense, Bosco's novel is perhaps one of the most complex and obscure he ever wrote.

On the other hand, *Antonin* (1952) is undeniably one of Bosco's best tales. Written for a younger audience and largely autobiographical, the story depicts life in a Provençal village at the turn of the century. We meet the Bénichats, a childless couple who used to keep young Antonin when his parents were away, Marie his young friend and Pataclé, the village drunk. But by far the most interesting characters are the two hunchback brothers, Barnabé and Cassius, owners of the general store and occasional moneylenders. Rumor has it that somewhere in the barrels of wine or in the coal reserve down in their cellar, a fabulous treasure lies hidden. The sight of these two men is enough to terrorize poor Antonin, who, inadvertently, discovers that Laïde, Bénichat's wife, is an alcoholic and has become dangerously indebted to the hunchbacks. With its well-drawn characters, attention to details and realistic dialogues, *Antonin* is perhaps the most Balzacian and one of the most entertaining of Bosco's stories.

Even more successful was *L'Enfant et la Rivière* (1953) which tells of the adventures of young Pascalet, who one day escapes the watchful eye of his beloved Aunt Martine to wander alone about the marshlands. After walking for hours, Pascalet discovers, hidden behind a forest of bulrushes, a small island. He immediately sets out to explore the new territory and stumbles upon a gypsy camp where Gatzo, a young boy, is being held captive. While the group is asleep, Pascalet frees Gatzo and the two leave on a small raft down the river. For days the two Provençal Tom Sawyer and Huck Finn hide in the woods and Gatzo

teaches Pascalet how to survive in nature. But their adventure must come to an end and Pascalet, realizing that Martine is worried, returns home and leaves Gatzo to travel on his own. The story shows another dimension of Bosco's artistic nature and reveals an innate talent for children's tales, which made him famous. It also successfully blends mystery with an impressionistic representation of nature and the river with its unpredictable moods and occasional floods. The book won him the Grand Prix National des Lettres.

But if childhood was a theme dear to Bosco, the world of spirits and ghosts, which he inherited from his mother, exerted such a powerful fascination that he felt compelled to write about it. *L'Antiquaire* (1954) takes place mostly in Marseilles and tells the story of young Baroudiel de la Herondaye and his encounter with two antique dealers fascinated with Greek and Roman civilizations. The story is complex and obscure. Its descriptive style, as well as the slow development of the plot and minimal dialogues, make it difficult to follow. Bosco is more successful when he describes the social aspect of Provençal life such as in *Les Balesta* (1956) where he represents the village of Trevignelles before the Industrial Revolution. Through a simple love story between Melchior and Ameline, Bosco shows that despite the class differences the inhabitants were basically happy: "They enjoyed a good drink, ate well, were born well, died not too badly and the race was healthy."[27]

In 1955, the Boscos decided to return to Provence. They bought a house in Cimiez, just above Nice and decorated it in a North African style to remind them of their former residence. They often attended the artistic events of the Côte d'Azur and renewed their acquaintance with their old friends. Bosco divided his time between reading his favorite authors, Theocritus, Virgil and Plotinus, and writing. Since his former children's tales had been successful, Bosco decided to please his public and he wrote *Le Renard dans l'Île* (1956). The story is a sequel to *L'Enfant et la Rivière* and begins when Martine adopts Gatzo and Brother Théopiste teaches him to write. During their stay on the island, Pascalet and Gatzo discover a mysterious animal that looks like a white fox who has the soul of a young girl trapped inside it. The two boys hunt the fox and Gatzo eventually kills it thereby freeing the spirit of the young girl. The following year, Bosco wrote *Le Chien Barboche,* a tale in which Tante Martine and Pascalet and their dog Barboche travel in a carriage to Pierrouré to visit Martine's cousins the Gloriots. Their journey is full of adventures for, while continuing on foot, they are

attacked by a pack of ferocious dogs and followed by a mysterious donkey, probably belonging to some gypsies. When they finally reach their destination their disappointment is great for the village, like the others they went through, is abandoned and the Gloriots have left.

When not in Nice, the Boscos traveled to Italy and Spain but especially to Lourmarin in the Lubéron where they would spend the summer months. Bosco met with his friends, poets Gabriel Audisio, Louis Brauquier, writers Edmonde Charles-Roux, André Chamson and painter Yves Brayer. Bosco loved to take long walks in the mountain in the company of his friends. There, in the silence of nature and the discreet presence of the ruins of a Romanesque church or a quaint medieval village, he found his inspiration. In *L'Epervier* (1963), Joachim Balesta, the last descendant of the family, returns to Pierrelousse, the village of his ancestors. But a long time has elasped since the last Balesta died and only two old inhabitants still remember them. Balesta meets the old maid Agathe, Prosper and Balagne the evil spirits, Fulbert the hunchback, Miralet the lutemaker and his daughter Mélanie, a beautiful and talented harpist, but no one can inform him about his ancestors. Searching through the local archives, Balesta finally learns of the existence of a certain Sabinus, Captain of the Epervier, a swashbuckler who died at sea fighting the Turks and the English during the napoleonic era. In the meantime, his presence and investigation into the village's past rekindles old feuds and Balesta becomes the object of the villagers' animosity. He is finally forced to leave so he returns home to the Riviera. One day during one of his walks on the beach he catches a glimpse of the Epervier.

Unlike Mistral and Daudet's, Bosco's art is hermetic and shows no concern for external or historical events. The social and political unrest of the late 1960s and the independence of Algeria, the forced exodus of the over one million French *pieds noirs* in 1962, certainly affected him but did not filter into his stories which he continued to write along the same themes and often with the same characters. In *Mon Compagnon des Songes* (1967), fifteen-year-old Pascalet leaves home for an excursion alone in Provence. His first stop is the village of Venoves, residence of old Eustache Lopy, one of his distant relatives. After a short journey by train, Pascalet arrives in the village and walks into the local café. There he meets a strange fellow by the name of Matthias who eventually takes him to Eustache Lopy's house. During the days that follow, Pascalet makes the acquaintance of Eustache's three sisters and learns that long ago there was another sister named Hortense whom Eustache

locked up for ten years because she was being courted by Matthias, a good-for-nothing fellow according to her brother. The locals did not know and thought Hortense had left the village. After ten years of imprisonment, Hortense died but the other sisters continued to remain silent. Disheartened, Pascalet finally leaves the village and heads back home. Later he learns that, shortly after his departure, Eustache shot and killed a man who was trying to climb his wall and went insane.

By now Bosco was the recipient of many literary prizes and honors. In 1965, he was awarded the Grand Prix Méditerranée, two years later he received the Prix de l'Académie du Vaucluse, and in 1968 the Grand Prix de l'Académie Française. Bosco wrote many prefaces for other writers, including one for a reprint of *Mireio*, and began to interest academics such as Jean Godin. Nevertheless, the French Academy did not solicit his candidature, which is not surprising because he neither paid the traditional visits to its distinguished members, nor mingled with influential literary critics. Like his predecessors Mistral and Daudet, Bosco remained indifferent to the Académie. Instead, he preferred to concentrate his efforts on his next story *Tante Martine* (1972) in which, to the list of already familiar characters such as Martine, Bargabot the fisherman and Béranger the shepherd, he added Saladin the Turk and Mache the young maid. But Bosco returned one last time to his former loves: Camargue and Greece. In *Le Récif* (1971), young Jerôme Moneval-Yssel settles on Liguset in Camargue, an isolated property he recently inherited from his father's cousin Markos, who disappeared in 1920. The memory of Markos pervades Liguset and with the help of his cousin's servants Séverine and Justine, Moneval tries to elucidate his unexplained disappearance. Searching the house he finds a notebook containing the unfinished story of an extraordinary journey to Greece. Intrigued, Doneval decides to follow in his cousin's footsteps and embarks for Greece. When Bosco died, in 1976, at home, he was working on *Une Ombre,* the story of Monneval-Yssel's voyage through Provence in the footsteps of his great-uncle who walked the same trails in 1850. The novel was published posthumously in 1978.

During his long career as a teacher and writer, Bosco had also been a frequent contributor to reviews such as *Cahiers du Sud, L'Astrado* and *Marseille* edited by Brauquier. After a few travel books such as *Pages Marocaines* (1948) and *Alger* (1950), he began to write down his souvenirs in a series of books such as *Un Oubli Moins Profond* (1961), *Le Chemin de Montclar* (1962) and *Le Jardin des Trinitaires* (1966). He was buried in the small graveyard of Lourmarin where Albert Camus

also lies. "La véritable Provence est une Provence grave," Bosco believed and his works illustrate this statement.[28] Provençal's famous gaiety and jovial spirits were, in his opinion, only a mask that hid a more solemn and melancholy nature. To truly understand Provence, Bosco argues one must remain silent, go beyond its visible manifestations and search for its spirit. Hence a necessary adaptation to a different dimension in which myth plays a role and time almost comes to a halt. In his novels, written in a classic style, action, as R. Sussex remarks, is "phenomenally slow" and takes place in the protagonist's vision more than in external events.[29] Bosco's art is, for the most part, hermetic and represents a personal spiritual quest. Except for his children's tales, his stories are difficult to read which explains why he never was as popular as Pagnol or Giono. The subject matters of his stories as well as his style remain profoundly influenced by the classics. Brauquier argued that sometimes Bosco wrote first in Latin and then translated his work into French. According to him, without knowledge of Latin one cannot fully understand Bosco.[30]

Endnotes

1. Henri Bosco, *Un Oubli moins Profond* (Paris: Gallimard, 1961) 15.
2. Apparently three were stillborn and the baby girl Marguerite died at ten months. Communication from Claude Girault, President of *L'Amitié Henri Bosco* to whom I am indebted for most biographical data concerning Bosco.
3. Jean Godin, *Le Sens du Mystère dans l'oeuvre de Henri Bosco* (Montréal: Presses de l'Université, 1966) 19.
4. "Elle avait l'imagination vive et puissante. De l'object le plus ordinaire, elle tirait des formes imprévues." Bosco, *Antonin* (Paris: Gallimard, 1965) 348.
5. "Le rêve incline l'esprit, chacun sait, à la bienveillance. Penser c'est mordre. Rêver c'est caresser de simples images..." Bosco, *Un Oubli moins Profond* 46.
6. "J'ai été ainsi élevé dans l'odeur de la terre, du blé et du vin nouveau." Bosco, *Antonin* (Paris: Gallimard, 1980) 16.
7. "Je puis même l'affirmer qu'il n' y a que cela qui compte pour moi, la campagne. J'en ai gardé le besoin et l'amour toute ma vie." Bosco, *Un Oubli moins Profond* 39.
8. "Ces histoires m'avaient tourné la tête. J'en ai rêvé pendant toute mon enfance. Bosco, *L'Habitant de Sivergues* (Paris: Gallimard, 1935) 145.
9. "Quand j'étais seul avec ma mère, qui faisait mitonner sa daube, nous rappelions tel événement dramatique où apparaissaient d'Artagnan, Anne d'Autriche et le terrible Cardinal de Richelieu. La cuisine en était transfigurée." Bosco, *Le Chemin de Montclar* (Paris: Gallimard, 1962) 58.

10. "Malheureusement, c'était plat." Bosco, *Antonin* 16.

11. "Je suis un homme des collines." Bosco, *Hyacinthe* (Paris: Gallimard, 1940) 20.

12. "Virgile, je crois, c'est le poète auquel, toutes proportions gardées, je ressemblerais le plus." Jean-Pierre Cauvin, *Henri Bosco et la Poétique du Sacré* (Paris: Klincksieck, 1974) 252.

13. "A quinze ans j'admirais déjà Mistral à l'égal d'Homère." Bosco, *Tableau de la Littérature Française: de Mme de Staël à Rimbaud* (Paris: Gallimard, 1974) 328.

14. "J'ai passé mon enfance à regarder, de ma fenêtre...le clocher de Maillane, et tout le pays chanté dans *Mireille* je l'ai eu pendant des années sous les yeux. Adolescent, je l'ai parcouru à pied et à chaque pas je trouvais le poète. Quand j'y reviens, je le retrouve encore; il a marqué le pays." Bosco 329.

15. "L'homme m'a séduit aussitôt. L'aspect en était imposant et familier. On nous l'a décrit quelquefois impérial et comme solaire; pourtant je ne l'ai jamais vu tel. Il avait de la grandeur, mais un acceuil si bienveillant, que cette majesté restait humaine. On pouvait l'aimer." Bosco 329.

16. "Il reste pour moi la plus haute figure d'homme qu'il m'ait été donné de rencontrer, l'homme complet, où tout fusionne...Vie, poésie, sagesse, sont en Mistral inséparables." Bosco 329.

17. "Je suis né sans doute dans les songes et pour les songes dont je vis."Bosco, *L'Epervier* (Paris: Gallimard, 1963) 309.

18. "Le plus grand poète provençal depuis Mistral." Cauvin, *Henri Bosco et la Poétique du Sacré* 254.

19. "Et j'ai lu. J'ai lu lentement, gravement, avec passion, depuis le coucher du soleil jusqu'à minuit. Lu presque sans interruption." Bosco, *Le Récif* (Paris: Gallimard, 1971) 20. "Pour nous Provençaux, ce livre c'est notre *Centaure*." Bosco wrote shortly after d'Arbaud's death. See Claude Girault in *Cahiers Henri Bosco* 35/36 (La Calade: Edisud, 1995): 32, 33.

20. Pour moi...Lourmarin est un lieu où souffle l'esprit, et cet esprit, je le sens dans ma chair, mon coeur, mon intelligence.Aussi chanterai-je encore cette place, ce bastion de poësie où la Grèce, Rome, la Provence, la France se mêlent d'une façon unique." Claude Girault, *Henri Bosco: Lettres à Noël Vesper* (Lourmarin, 1986) 2.

21. "Il n'y a pas de littérature pour moi sans poésie." Cauvin, *Henri Bosco et la Poétique du Sacré* 2.

22. Cauvin 247.

23. "L'oeuvre du romancier, c'est un pouvoir de fascination exercé sur le lecteur par l'auteur en état d'hallucination." Cauvin 235.

24. Cauvin 234.

25. "L'enfant ne vit, comme nous, dans un monde logique (ou qui paraît tel), mais dans un décor inventé...l'on n'y est pas devant, mais au milieu des choses..." Bosco, *Antonin* 84

26. "Il est de cette race de Méridionaux silencieux, comme il y en a tant." Louis Brauquier, "Bosco le silencieux," *Les Nouvelles Littéraires* November 14, 1968, 6.

27. "On y buvait sec, on y mangeait gras, on y naissait bien, et l'on n'y mourait pas trop mal. La race était saine." Bosco, *Les Balesta* (Paris: Gallimard, 1956) 35.

28. Robert Ytier, *Henri Bosco ou L'Amour de la Vie* (Lyons: Aubanel,1996) 185.

29. R.T. Sussex, *Henri Bosco, poet-novelist* (Christchurch: University of Canterbury, 1966) 11.

30. "Sans le latin, on ne comprend rien à Bosco. Toute son oeuvre est traduite du latin et du grec. A tel point d'ailleurs qu'il écrit parfois le latin d'abord." Brauquier, "Bosco le silencieux" 6.

Five

Marcel Pagnol

"He had a wonderful and God-given talent for storytelling. He knew it and used it with exceptional virtuosity," Raymond Castans remembers.[1] Marcel Pagnol is another child of Provence with a passion for telling stories. His art is deeply rooted in the cultural atmosphere of Marseilles at the turn of the century. "I was born in the town of Aubagne under the Garlaban mountain crowned with goats," Pagnol writes in *La Gloire de mon Père* in a way which is very reminiscent of Arène's introduction in *Jean des Figues*.[2] Aubagne is a small town some ten miles east of Marseilles, and at the time the Pagnols lived Rue Barthélemy where, on February 28, 1895 at five o'clock in the afternoon Marcel came into being. A year before, Mrs. Pagnol had given birth to her first son named Maurice but the baby died at four months of age. Mr. Joseph Pagnol's family came from the small town of Valréas, near Montélimar, where, since the sixteenth century, they had worked as gunsmiths and cardboard manufacturers. André Pagnol, Marcel's grandfather, was a

Marcel Pagnol 1895–1974 (Photograph Editions de Fallois, Paris).

small but strong man with eyes that shone like ripe olives, as he recalls. A stonecutter by trade, he married and lived for some time in nearby Vaison-la-Romaine, and then moved to Marseilles. He had six children including Joseph, Marcel's father. Like his brother Adolph and sister Josephine, Joseph became an *instituteur* or elementary school teacher and, after studying in Aix, obtained his first position in Aubagne in 1889. In 1893, Joseph married Augustine-Pauline Lansot, an eighteen-year-old seamstress from Marseilles. There was no religious ceremony but Augustine, brought up in the Catholic tradition, later managed to have her son Marcel secretly baptized.

Augustine never knew her father who had left his native Normandy and settled in Marseilles. There he married a local woman and worked as a mechanic on board ships. He died when Pauline was only one year old. When Marcel was a child, Aubagne was a small town of about ten thousand people, "nestled on the banks of the Huveaune and linked to Marseilles and Toulon by a dusty road. People there fired tiles, manufactured bricks and jugs, stuffed sausages called *boudins* and *andouilles*."[3] Leather and *santons* or little clay figurines completed the local economy. But Pagnol did not live there for long. Two years later, in 1897, his father asked to be transferred to Marseilles.

Life in the big Mediterranean City was certainly more appealing and exciting. André Suarès, another writer native of the city, describes it as a "midday blaze," inhabited by a race of proud and independent people, heirs of the Greek civilization.[4] "To get a true understanding of

the city," he correctly remarks, "one must never forget Greece."[5] Indeed, Suarès was right. Founded by Greeks from Phocéa 600 BC, Marseilles played an important role in the ancient world and Aristotle devoted a book (unfortunately lost) to it. During Pagnol's childhood the city was a booming port. It imported copra, sugar cane, refined them into oil and sugar, and exported them back to Africa. Marseilles had more than one hundred soap factories, and the oil refineries alone employed approximately 11,000 people.[6] Candle making was also an important activity. Between 1870 and 1914 the population almost doubled from 313, 000 to 650,000, an increase largely due to the arrival of a new contingent of Italians.[7] The city could boast of illustrious people like Greek explorer Pithéas, politician Adolphe Thiers, caricaturist Honoré Daumier and playwright Edmond Rostand. It was there that four years before Pagnol's birth, poet Arthur Rimbaud passed away.

The Pagnols first lived a few miles inland in the Saint-Loup neighborhood, on the road to Aubagne, but in 1900 they moved downtown, first to Rue Tivoli, and then to Rue Terrusse, near the little hill known as La Plaine-Saint-Michel. During the next two decades, the Pagnols moved again several times but always remained in the same area. The family now counted another boy, Paul, born in 1898, as well as Germaine, the young sister, born in 1902. To escape the summer heat, the Pagnols, like many Marseillais, spent their vacation in the country. In 1904, they rented a house in the small village of La Treille perched on a hill midway between Marseilles and Aubagne. It is there that Pagnol for the first time discovered nature, not so much the life of farmers, since land there was barren and water rare, but "the life of the hills," as Jacques Bens shrewdly remarks.[8] Those desolate and rocky plateaus, somewhat reminiscent of Giono's high country, were almost deserted save for a few families who managed to eke out a living hunting rabbits, *bartavelles* or partridges, and occasionally wild boar. It was there that Lili (David Magnan), a village boy, revealed to Pagnol the secret life of this rugged country, teaching him how to read tracks, lay snares, find hidden springs, and identify every bird and plant. Uncle Jules and his wife were habitual guests and their lively characters added to the jovial atmosphere of the household. A native of southern Languedoc, Uncle Jules rolled his "r"s and his conservative Catholic upbringing often conflicted with that of Mr. Pagnol, liberal and agnostic like most school teachers under the Third Republic. Jules was also a wine connoisseur and always accompanied his meals with a good bottle which Mr. Pagnol, with his Puritan views on alcohol, disapproved. Those

summer days spent in the fascinating hills awakened Pagnol's sensual nature and nurtured his artistic imagination for the rest of his life. The world he discovered in the small and inconspicuous village of La Treille furnished him with all the necessary ingredients for his fiction and explains his later enthusiasm for the works of Giono.

As soon as summer was over, the Pagnols regained their apartment in town and life in the big city resumed its course. In 1905, Pagnol began to attend the Grand Lycée (now Lycée Thiers). In spite of his having taught himself reading at a very early age, Pagnol's early years in school were not particularly brilliant. In fact, his records show that he was a rather mediocre student who, like many of his friends, showed more interest in games and practical jokes than in curricular activities. However, at around the age of sixteen, his grades improved. At this time his French and Latin teacher was Emile Ripert, a *Félibre* and poet who introduced Pagnol to Virgil but also to modern writers such as playwright Edmond Rostand, the author of the famous *Cyrano de Bergerac*, himself a former student of the Grand Lycée. Pagnol's scholastic efforts did not diminish his sense of humor, which he shared with classmates Yves Bourde, whose family also spent vacation in La Treille, Fernand Avierinos, and Albert Cohen, the future novelist. Among Pagnol's favorite authors at the time were Dickens, Shakespeare, Daudet and Virgil. Pagnol wrote verse in French and some of his poems were published in the local review *Massilia* (June 1910). He loved opera and the theater and regularly attended plays. In July 1912, Pagnol passed his *baccalauréat* exams in Philosophy and the year after he entered, in the same lycée, *khâgne*, a prep class for the Ecole Normale Supérieure, the famous teacher training college in Paris. Early in 1914, Pagnol with his friend Jean Ballard started a bimonthly review called *Fortunio.* But the war broke out and the review ceased publication after six editions. It resurfaced later and was baptized *Les Cahiers du Sud* (1925–67).

Life at home took a tragic turn with the death of Mrs. Pagnol in 1910, following complications after the birth of her third child René. Mr. Pagnol gave up his position in the state system and began working for private institutions. In 1912, he remarried Madeleine Julien. The death of his beloved mother was a heavy blow to Pagnol and his father's remarriage did not improve the situation. He felt estranged and contemplated living on his own but in December 1914 he was drafted and sent to Nice. Fortunately, after five months, medical authorities there judged his health too fragile and declared him inapt for military service. This unexpected decision precipitated Pagnol's teaching career.

During the war he first worked as *maître d'internat,* like Daudet and Arène before him, in Digne, and the following year, moved to Tarascon to teach English. While in Tarascon, Pagnol also attended classes at the University of Montpellier and, in 1915, he graduated with a *licence* in English. Pagnol was now financially independent and eager to lead a life of his own.

For some time he had been seeing Simone Collin whom he had first met at his father's home when she came to pick up her sister, his father's pupil, for English lessons. Through a friend, Pagnol's father had learned of his son's "immoral" relationship with Simone and was outraged. To show his moral earnestness, Marcel proposed to marry Simone but his father refused to give his consent. Nevertheless, Pagnol was in love and in 1916, he turned twenty-one which meant he no longer needed parental authorization. The ceremony took place in March in a Protestant church since Simone was Protestant. Soon after, in the summer, the young couple left for the small town of Pamiers in the Pyrénées where Pagnol had found a teaching position. In 1919, they came back to Provence, Pagnol having obtained a new post in Lycée Mignet in Aix. The following year they were back in Marseilles where he taught in the annex of Lycée Thiers.

These early years were difficult, for Pagnol's true ambition was to become a writer. He asked to be transferred to Paris where he thought he had better chances of making his dream come true. In 1922, and not without some apprehension, he accepted a position there as an English teacher at the famous Lycée Condorcet. "Paris, which I imagined as an anthill in the rain, scared me," he later confessed.[9] Pagnol considered himself lucky because this was normally an end-of-career position but he had benefited from the help of a superintendent who convinced educational authorities that Pagnol had a promising teaching career in front of him and needed to be in Paris to prepare himself for the *agrégation,* which could later qualify him for a college position. For a few months, Marcel and Simone lived in a small dingy hotel but as soon as Simone found a job as a secretary for the Lycée their situation improved and they moved into an apartment near the school. The Pagnols were not without contacts in Paris. Paul Nivoix, a Marseillais friend, had also recently moved there and introduced them to a host of writers and artists among whom playwright Marcel Achard, a young Belgian journalist named Georges Simenon, and Gabriel Boissy. The latter, editor of *Comoedia,* a theater revue, asked Pagnol to contribute a few articles and the latter was happy to oblige. In the meantime, *Fortunio* resumed its

publication but the editorship was now in the hands of Jean Ballard in Marseilles who soon took the leading role. Pagnol remained in charge of the drama criticism until 1925 when, relationships with Ballard being at their worst, he chose to resign.

Life in the City of Lights and contacts with the art world fused Pagnol's literary imagination. Besides reviews and articles he and Nivoix wrote a play, *Tonton*. It was first performed in Marseilles in July 1924 and, in spite of its mediocre success (20 performances), brought the authors more money than they had expected, which encouraged them in their pursuit. Together the two friends wrote *Les Marchands de Gloire* (1925) and *Un Direct au Coeur* performed in Lille (1926). Encouraged by the small success of his plays and supported by his friends of *Les Moins de Trente Ans*, a small circle of young actors and playwrights, which counted among its members Paul Vialar, Pagnol decided to write fulltime and, in the spring of 1926, he took a leave of absence without pay from the Lycée. Pagnol and his friends wanted to reform drama but they refused to be assimilated with the Théâtre des Boulevards, and held a position midway between the traditional theater and "the empire of popular entertainment."[10] His circle of friends was slowly growing larger and now included writer Blaise Cendrars and actor Henri Chomette (future movie director René Clair).

Pagnol wrote alone now and began to introduce Provence to his audience. *Jazz* was played first in the Grand Théâtre of Monte Carlo and a few weeks later on December 21, 1926 at the Théâtre des Arts in Paris. In the major roles were his friends Pierre Blanchard, Harry Baur and Orane Demazis. The story takes place in Aix-en-Provence. Blaise is a Greek professor who hopes to be appointed to the Sorbonne for his lifelong work on an anonymous manuscript entitled *Phaeton* whose authorship he attributes to Plato. Unfortunately recent scholarship has just proven Blaise's theory mistaken. The news is a great shock to Blaise whose hopes of promotion are now nil. His future plans are shattered, and to avoid being ridiculed, he chooses to resign. Forgetting professors and students, Blaise decides to change his life and for the first time contemplates getting married. Following the promptings of his heart, represented on the stage by a young man, he proposes to Cécile Boissier, one of his most promising students. Surprised yet flattered, Cécile accepts and marriage plans are made. This irks Stepanovich, a young Yugoslavian student in love with Cécile, who plucks up his courage and proposes to her. Once again Blaise is defeated and, deeply depressed, shoots himself.

The audience applauded but critics were divided. The play, reminiscent of Daudet's novel *L'Immortel,* contains some of the themes dear to Pagnol which he later developed in his works, such as school life and the serious and tragic sides of love. Harry Baur played the role of Blaise and remained one of Pagnol's long time actors and friends. Since 1925, Pagnol and his wife Simone lived separately. His wife was very religious and did not want a divorce, which was then still difficult to obtain and so they preferred to live apart. Pagnol was now involved in a relationship with Orane Demazis, the actress who played the role of Cécile. Her real name was Marie-Louise Burgard. Demazis was a very independent woman and she and Pagnol never really lived together. In 1933, she bore him a son, Jean-Pierre, but shortly after they parted ways.

Topaze, Pagnol's next play, met with triumphal success and from October 9, 1928 ran continuously for two and half years. Set in Paris, the play revolves around the adventures of a dedicated and moral teacher named Topaze. Topaze is dismissed from school because he refuses to pass a student, Baroness Pitart-Vergniolles' son. Muche, the school principal, always ready to accommodate wealthy and influential parents, is outraged at Topaze's determination and fires him. What hurts Topaze the most is that he is in love with the principal's daughter Ernestine for whom he often grades exams. Topaze leaves his position without much regret however and begins looking for a new job. Soon he meets beautiful Susie and Castel-Benac her supervisor who offers him a job as a salesperson. As time goes by, Topaze becomes aware that his boss is using him for shady but profitable deals but, this time, he overcomes his feelings of shame and disgust and fights back. He applies his accute business acumen and analytical skills to commerce, beats his boss at his own game, puts him out of business and, in doing so, wins Susie's heart.

The first part of the play contains a sharp criticism of the French educational system and shows the dangerous consequences of moral idealism in the real world. Both the public and critics acclaimed the play as a masterpiece. "I heard Molière and Marivaux applaud in the background," wrote Maurice Rostand.[11] *Topaze* was subsequently performed in all the capitals of Europe and as far as Quebec and New York with similar success. In 1932, it was brought to the screen under the direction of Louis Gasnier and with Louis Jouvet in the leading role. In 1936, Pagnol shot his own version with Arnaudy and, in 1950, another one with Fernandel.

Life in Paris was certainly rich and exciting for a young and

ambitious writer such as Pagnol, but inevitably, like for his predecessors Daudet and Rostand, once the initial enthusiasm was over, a feeling of homesickness soon manifested itself. "I would dream about a
happy people of fishermen and women fishmongers...once again I
smelled the aroma of long and narrow stores where, hidden in the shad-
ows, lay rolls of moorings, sails, folded on shelves, and big copper
lanterns hung from the ceiling. I imagined again the small shady cafés
along the wharves and the young Marseillaises behind their seafood
stands. And with a lot of affection I began to write the story of Marius," Pagnol remembers.[12] Pagnol also declared that it was his friend
Pierre Blanchard who encouraged him to choose Marseilles as a setting for a play.[13] Marius had, in fact, been in Pagnol's mind for some
time and he had jotted down a few lines before he even began writing
Topaze. One may wonder what would have become of *Marius*, if it had
been performed before *Topaze* and if the local color would have been
accepted just the same. In any case, the success of the latter play certainly conditioned and prepared the Parisian public.

Marius was originally written for a Marseillais audience and for
the Alcazar of Marseilles, a vaudeville theater in the city center where
artists such as Alida Rouffe and standup comic Fernand Contandin (Fernandel) performed. It was Mr. Franck, the director who, seeing the success of Topaze, convinced Pagnol to have the play first performed in
the capital Pagnol did not adapt his play for a Parisian audience and
when it premiered at the Théâtre de Paris on March 9, 1929 its local
color was received with mixed feelings. While adding a picturesque
touch, Marseillais idiom and accent were not always understood, not to
mention passages when actors resorted to Provençal. But the play was
moving, the dialogues well written, and finally Raimu's performance in
the role of César so perfect, that is was a veritable triumph.

Pagnol had hired Provençal actor Raimu (Jules Muraire) for the
role of Panisse the sail maker, but Raimu, with his keen artistic instinct
felt that he must play César and Pagnol accepted. For the role of Marius, Pagnol had thought of Blanchard who played in *Jazz*. Blanchard
was a *pied noir* and had lived in Marseilles for three years but he was
not available, so Pagnol gave the role to Alsacian born actor Pierre Fresnay who had been stationed in Marseilles during his military service.
At first Raimu was vehemently opposed to the idea, arguing that it made
no sense for César to have a son with a Northern accent but Pagnol
finally convinced him that Fresnay was a good actor who could be taught
to imitate the Marseillais accent and Raimu finally accepted. So Fresnay

took Marseillais lessons and worked for two weeks in Marseilles. Alida Rouffe from the Alcazar who Pagnol had cast in *Tonton* played the role of Honorine and Fernand Charpin the role of Panisse. Orane Demazis played Fanny but her accent also presented a problem. Pagnol invented a North African childhood for her like that of Orane. According to his contemporaries and co-workers, Pagnol listened to the remarks of his favorite actors and often wrote parts to suit them. His plays, like his films, were the results of a team effort.

Marius is set in Marseilles on the Vieux Port in the 1920s. César, a widower and his twenty-two-year old son Marius are the proud owners of *Le Bar de la Marine,* a small café on the harbor. Fanny, secretly in love with Marius since she was a child, works with her mother Honorine, also a widow, and sells shellfish from a stand on the harbor. Panisse, a fifty-year-old sail maker and widower proposes to Fanny. To make Marius jealous, Fanny pretends she is interested in Panisse's proposal but confesses to her mother that she loves Marius. Marius is jealous but hesitates to declare his love to Fanny because since childhood his only dream has been to sail around the world. However, Fanny finally tells Marius she is in love with him and the latter soon gives up his dream and they began planning their wedding. As the months go by, Honorine discovers that the relationship between Fanny and Marius is no longer platonic and, outraged, informs César who in turn talks to Marius. Marius promises to marry Fanny. But love cannot destroy Marius' dream and realizing that he will never be happy until he has sailed around the world, Fanny encourages him to board a ship and Marius leaves without telling his father.

The play ran continuously for three years totaling more than one thousand performances, breaking all records. *Marius* showed all the themes that haunted Pagnol, namely the tragic side of love, the problem of children born outside wedlock, filial duty and above all paternal love. There is a definite tragic dimension to all of his stories but they are balanced with subtle humor and sharp dialogues which especially delighted Provençals and Marseillais. Despite Fresnay's effort and good performance, his accent was unfortunately far from native. Pagnol was a talented playwright but the success of his plays (and films) is also due to the immense talent of his actors, especially Raimu and Fernandel.

After the triumph of *Marius,* Pagnol's group of friends widened considerably and included poet Jean Cocteau, and filmmaker Jean Renoir. His love life was taking a new turn and for a year Pagnol had

been living with a young English dancer Kitty Murphy in his newly acquired windmill at Ignières (Normandy). Kitty bore him his first son whom they named Jacques. The sequel to *Marius* was written in a few months and entitled *Fanny*. Casting, however, had given him great difficulties. Following a serious argument, Léon Volterra, director of the theater, had fired Raimu. Pagnol hoped for a compromise and tried to appease Volterra's anger but to no avail and he was forced to look elsewhere. Harry Baur, who previously acted in *Jazz,* accepted the role of César. Alida Rouffe (Honorine) injured in a train accident, was hospitalized and unable to take the role. To replace her, Pagnol was fortunate enough to find another talented actress and authentic Marseillaise in the person of Mrs. Chabert from the Alcazar. To make things worse, Fresnay was not available. Marius was played by Marseillais Berval. Fortunately, Orane Demazis was not engaged elsewhere and agreed to play the role of Fanny. *Fanny* was first performed at the Théâtre de Paris on December 5, 1931.

The story begins some months after Marius' departure. César and Fanny finally receive the long awaited letter from Marius in which he reassures them that his life on board is fine and that he enjoys being part of the oceanography expedition around the world. César immediately proceeds to answer his son's letter. In the meantime, Panisse asks Honorine for Fanny's hand and she accepts. However, soon afterwards Fanny tells her mother that she is expecting a child and that Marius is the father. Fanny also informs Panisse and César. Panisse, a fifty-three-year-old widower, is only too happy to finally have the son that his first wife could not give him, and César rejoices in the idea of being a grandfather and godfather. Since Marius is going to be at sea for at least two more years, Fanny, who does not want to bear her child out of wedlock, marries Panisse and promises to be a good wife. The secret is kept between the small circle of friends but Marius, during a short visit, understands that he is Césariot's real father and requests custody of his son. Panisse tells Fanny she is free to go back to Marius but refuses to give up his son. Finally, César interferes and argues that while Marius is the biological father, the real father, the one who raised the child, remains Panisse. Shamed and reluctant to disagree, Marius leaves again.

The trilogy was completed in 1936 with *César*. Twenty years have elapsed and the play begins with Panisse on his deathbed. Césariot, Fanny's son, a student at the prestigious Ecole Polytechnique in Paris, is on break at home. Fanny finally tells her son that her real father is Marius. Césariot, who had often wondered about the age difference

between Panisse and Fanny is not totally surprised and asks César for more information. The latter confirms Fanny's story and confides that the last he heard of Marius he was working as a mechanic in Toulon, still single but unfortunately often seen in the company of petty crooks. Césariot secretly goes to Toulon and pays his father a visit, without revealing his true identity. A few days later, Césariot meets Marius again at a car dealer's in Marseilles and this time tells him that he is his son. Fanny confesses to Marius that she still loves him and is willing to marry him. Marius hesitates because she is now wealthy and is afraid people will talk, but finally accepts. Pagnol was by now a successful playwright and the trilogy brought him international fame, although *Fanny* and *César* were not as masterly done, as *Marius*.

Like many of his friends, Pagnol began to take more interest in the new movie industry. Soon after *The Jazz Singer* (1927) and *The Lights of New York* (1928), the first talkies reached Paris and the French followed in the footsteps of the Americans. In 1929, André Hugon shot *Les Trois Masques* and in 1930 René Clair *Sous les Toits de Paris*. All the great companies, Paramount, Metro, Fox and Universal, were shooting talkies. *Jean de la Lune* by Marcel Achard and directed by Jean Choux with Madeleine Renaud and Michel Simon was a fantastic commercial success. "It exploded like a bomb. The film played for twenty-five consecutive weeks," Pagnol recalls.[14] In the spring of 1930, Blanchard came back from London raving about *Broadway Melody* and encouraged Pagnol to go see it. The next day Pagnol was sitting in the balcony in the London Palladium and watched the film twice. His decision was made: "From now on cinema is the business of playwrights...to remain silent is a handicap like limping.... A new art form is born...I will no longer write for the theater. I shall write films."[15] The new invention of sound movies fascinated Pagnol and he thought it was the end of the theater.

Pagnol subsequently met American producer Robert Kane who was in Paris to build studios for Paramount. According to Pagnol, Kane wanted to buy the rights for *Marius* but he spoke almost no French and had no idea of what Provence was which left Pagnol wondering about the outcome of the film. Furthermore, Kane intended do to things the American way, hire well-known actors, make cuts and change a few scenes. Pagnol accepted but requested that Kane use the same actors as in the play, and asked for the supervision of the directing, and royalties in the sales. After long discussions Kane finally agreed and hired Alexander Korda, a Hungarian born American, to direct the film. In exchange, Pagnol agreed to let Kane shoot a Swedish and a German

version of *Marius* simultaneously, as he pleased. Thus Pagnol, somewhat befuddled by the strange situation, came to the studios every day in Joinville and watched step by step the shooting of three different versions of his Marseillais film. "I was rather surprised to meet every day in the studio restaurant, three César, three Fanny, three Marius and three Escartefigue, who could not say two words to one another except *gin, à votre santé* and *"s'il vous plaît,"* Pagnol remembers with his usual humor.[16]

Korda understood Pagnol better than Kane and shot *Marius* with dialogues in French by Pagnol in five weeks. Pagnol then associated himself with a French production company Braunberger-Richebé and worked with director Marc Allégret to bring *Fanny* to the screen. But this time he managed to keep the same cast with Raimu and Fresnay and shot the film partially on location in Marseilles. Marc Allégret, who had worked with Raimu in *Le Blanc et le Noir,* directed and the film came out in 1932. Pagnol found himself financially able to produce his own movies. He hired Roger Lion to direct the film adaptation of *Un Direct au Coeur* (1932) and Marseillais Richebé for *L'Agonie des Aigles* (1933), but these were failures. In the meantime, he had acquired enough knowledge of the techniques involved in the making of sound films and, in 1933, he created his company *Les Auteurs Associés* and launched a journal *Les Cahiers du Film.* He also bought a mill near Paris where he shot *Le Gendre de Monsieur Poirier* (1933) adapted from the play of Emile Aughier and Jules Sandeau. In 1934, the company was renamed *Les Films Marcel Pagnol* and the following year Pagnol built his own studios, but this time in Marseilles, Impasse des Peupliers (on the Prado) bought a few cinemas and equipped them for sound projection. Jean Renoir often visited him there. In 1932, Pagnol's brother Paul, who suffered from epilepsy, died in a Belgium hospital while he was undergoing an operation. Because of his handicap Paul had abandoned his studies in agriculture and lived on a plot of land near La Treille where he raised goats. Pagnol's affair with Kitty Murphy had recently ended and he seized the opportunity to resume his relationship with Demazis.

The cinema did not put an end to Pagnol's lifelong interest in literature. On the contrary, he began to turn to fiction for inspiration and in 1932 wrote to Giono asking permission to adapt some of this novels to the screen. The choice of Giono was not the result of a hasty decision, for since his first novels, Giono had been one of his favorite authors. Pagnol contacted Giono who accepted to participate in the enterprise and was to receive 6 percent of the benefits. Pagnol bought

several acres of land in the hills behind La Treille where his brother Paul lived, and set up his studios. He began with *Jofroi* adapted from Giono's short story "Jofroi de La Maussan." Up in the high plateaus around Manosque, old Jofroi sells his land to Fonse but keeps his house. When Fonse begins to tear up peach trees on his new property Jofroi threatens him with a gun and forbids him to touch his trees. Fonse argues that they are no longer his but Jofroi refuses to listen and, in the following days attempts several times to commit suicide, first by jumping from his roof, then by lying on the middle of the road expecting to be run over by cars...until, finally, one day he dies of a heart attack. Fonse resumes his work in the field but, in memory of Jofroi, leaves a few trees standing. The cast was composed of Marseillais Vincent Scotto (Jofroi) who wrote the music for *Fanny,* with Henri Poupon and Charles Blavette in the principal roles. Pagnol remained faithful to Giono, but his version contains more humor and comic scenes. The film was a success and Scotto became immediately famous.

A year after, Pagnol shot *Angèle* adapted from *Un de Baumugnes* with Jean Servais in the role of Albin, Orane Demazis as Angèle and Blavette, Delmont, Poupon, and for the first time Fernandel in the role of Saturnin. In 1937, for the production of *Regain,* Pagnol hired his childhood friends Marius Brouquier, a stone mason, to build a small village in the hills behind LaTreille, the ruins of which still stand today. Fernandel played the part of Gédémus and Demazis that of Arsule. The actors Poupon, Blavette, Delmont, Milly Mathis, and Jean Castan also participated. Critics found the film too long (2 hours). In 1938, Pagnol filmed *La Femme du Boulanger* adapted from *Jean le Bleu.* The exterior scenes were shot in the village of Le Castellet near Toulon. Raimu plays Aimable Castanier, a baker whose young wife Aurélie (played by Ginette Leclerc) leaves him for a handsome shepherd. Too depressed to work, Castanier stops baking bread. Soon the local population feels concerned since there is no baker for miles around. However, there is hope, for a farmer spotted his wife and the young man on a small island in the marshes and the *instituteur* along with the priest speak with them to convince Aurélie to come back. At the sight of the vicar, the sinful shepherd is afraid and flees, and finally Aurélie returns home. Castanier forgives her. The film was a triumph and in 1940 received an American Oscar for best foreign film.

Giono was undoubtedly a little jealous of the success of Pagnol's films and not always satisfied with his free interpretations of his novels. In fact, he stopped participating in Pagnol's screenplays very early

on. This soon created a problem for Pagnol who refused to pay Giono his six percent. Pagnol had also published the dialogues of the movies he made from Giono's novels under his own name and Giono complained. In 1941, the disagreement had to be settled before a court of law in Marseilles. The contract stipulated that Giono was entitled to six percent if he participated, which he never did, and Pagnol won. This affair put a temporary end to the relationship between Pagnol and Giono but their friendship resumed soon after the war and their previous disagreements were forgotten. A member of the Académie Française since 1946, Pagnol encouraged Giono to present his candidacy. Giono was thankful but he preferred the Académie Goncourt. However, Pagnol was instrumental in obtaining for him the Prix de Monaco in 1953. Giono's novels had also the merit of turning the attention of Pagnol inland to rural Provence.

But Giono was not the only Provençal author that inspired Pagnol. In 1934, he turned to Daudet, also a favorite author of his, and produced *Tartarin*. The film, directed by Raymond Bernard was played by Raimu and Charpin, and the script written by Pagnol. Critics were disappointed and Pagnol waited until 1954 to return to Daudet and shoot his *Lettres de mon Moulin* with Rellys and Fernand Sardou which, unfortunately, did not fare better. But Daudet had also inspired him and Pagnol shot *Merlusse* (1935), adapted from a short story he wrote for *Fortunio*. The story, reminiscent of Daudet's *Le Petit Chose,* deals with the loneliness of the students and teachers. In the principal roles were Poupon and Jean Castan. At Christmas time and in the Lycée where Merlusse, the one eyed *maître d'internat*, has recently been appointed, most students leave to spend their vacation with their families except a dozen of them, literally abandoned to their fate by their uncaring parents. Merlusse's homely appearance and his strict observance of discipline make him the object of hatred among the students. To please the principal, Merlusse accepts to replace a professor who was sick and agrees to look over the students over Christmas. But behind Merlusse's reserved attitude and austere look, hides a sensitive person who, while the boys are asleep, goes to town to buy the boys presents which he places in their boots. The next morning the students are bewildered but delighted and in turn place some of their favorite toys in Merlusse's shoes. But Merlusse's generosity is against the rules and, summoned in the principal's office for what he thinks will be his dismissal, Merlusse is, to his great surprise, rewarded with a promotion.

Cigalon (1935) shot in La Treille, is perhaps one of the funniest,

but paradoxically least known, of Pagnol's movies. It is the story of a chef Cigalon (Arnaudy) who after having worked in the best restaurants of Marseilles for many years where he prepared gourmet dishes, finally opens his own restaurant in a village nearby. But Cigalon is not an ordinary character (he is, in fact, a cross between Tartarin and César), and he refuses to serve customers! He believes that most of them know nothing about real *cuisine* and cannot pay full homage to his dishes. Therefore, he prefers to cook for himself. But when Mrs. Toffi (Marguerite Chabert) a former laundry owner, informs him of her decision to open her own restaurant, one that will actually serve customers. Cigalon is insulted but prepares himself to take on the challenge and Mrs. Toffi promises that if Cigalon makes more money than she does with his customers, she will accept to marry him.

The village soon bustles with activity and competition between the two restaurants is stiff. One day a Count (Henri Poupon) arrives in the village, driven by his chauffeur, and Cigalon does his best to entice him into his restaurant. The customer hesitates but finally comes in, sits down at a table and orders the most expensive dishes. Cigalon is happy to have found a customer who honors his creations and serves him like a king, but when it comes to paying the bill the supposedly wealthy customer, his appetite satisfied, confesses that, unfortunately, he has no money. Cigalon becomes angry and violent but calms himself down and calls the *gendarmes*. After a brief inquiry, the *gendarmes* are ready to take the crook away but Cigalon realizes that he is going to lose his challenge and look ridiculous, so he devises a plan. A few moments later the police are gone and Cigalon shakes the gentleman's hand in presence of Mrs. Toffi and the villagers and the latter makes sure to thank him for the excellent dinner and pays him (with Cigalon's own money) in cash. Cigalon is happy and proposes to Mrs. Toffi who accepts. For some obscure reason the film failed to entertain the critics. It is true that Raimu or Fernandel, the best actors of the time were engaged elsewhere. "*Cigalon* n'a jamais fait rire que moi. Mais beaucoup," commented Pagnol.[17]

Le Schpountz (1937) fared a little better and plays Fernandel in the role of Irénée, a young and naive man employed by his uncle (Charpin) in the village's grocery store. When a movie director drives into town with his team of actors and technicians, Irénée, utterly convinced of his immense dramatic talent, believes that this is the chance of a lifetime and immediately befriends the troop. He attends all scenes and later shows the actors around town always boasting his amazing talents. Tired

of the young man's vanity Françoise (Demazis) the screenwriter, and her friends, decide to teach him a lesson. They tell him that, indeed, he is a born actor and offer him a contract for a film to be shot in Paris. Irénée's vanity is piqued and in spite of his uncle's warnings, leaves for Paris. After a series of unsuccessful attempts at acting, Irénée soon realizes that he has been the object of a practical joke. However, he is happy to find a job as a set technician. Irénée does his job well and over the months the movie director discovers in him a real talent for comedy and gives him a trial role. Success is immediate and before long Irénée becomes a star and marries Françoise.

In 1938, Pagnol opened his new and bigger studios in Marseilles, Rue Jean Mermoz. He also bought *Le Chatelet,* a nearby cinema, and, in 1939, built his own, which he baptized *Le César.* His love life was as unhappy as ever and he ended a five-year relationship with Yvonne Pouperon who worked for his studios and who gave him a daughter, Francine. The following year Pagnol met Josette Day who, with Raimu and Fernandel, played the leading role in his next film *La Fille du Puisatier.* The story takes place at the eve of World War II. Pascal Amoretti (Raimu), a well digger by trade and widower is raising his five daughters alone. Felipe (Fernandel), his apprentice, is secretly in love with Patricia (Josette Day), the eldest daughter, but the latter loves Jacques Mazel, a young pilot. At the end of the war Felipe comes home with a medal but Jacques is missing in action. Patricia is now pregnant and Amoretti informs the Mazels that their son is the father. They are outraged and refuse to believe him. Amoretti's sister offers Patricia a room in her house in Fuveau, where soon a son is born. Over the months, Amoretti and the Mazels begin to love the baby and the latter begin to see a resemblance to their son Jacques who miraculously resurfaces and marries Patricia. In the meantime, another one of Amoretti's daughters falls in love with Felipe. The film was a success.

In 1941, Pagnol bought La Buzine, a small 19th-century mansion on a hill facing La Treille, where Edmond Rostand, one of its former residents, had written *L'Aiglon.* He lived and worked there with Josette Day until 1943, when they separated. Pagnol, who had divorced his wife in 1941, was now often seen in the company of a young actress by the name of Jacqueline Bouvier (no relation to Jacqueline Kennedy) and in 1945 the two got married. Jacqueline was twenty years old and her parents originally came from the Cévennes but she usually spent her summer vacation in Provence. Pagnol had met her in Paris where she went to drama school and performed in a couple of movies. In 1947,

Jacqueline gave birth to a son, Frédéric, and, in 1954, to a daughter, Estelle, who unfortunately died at the age of two. The two names inevitably recall Mistral.

Jacqueline became his favorite actress and played all the leading roles in his films beginning with *Naïs* (1945) directed by Raymond Leboursier and adapted from a short story by Emile Zola called *Naïs Micoulin*. Toine (Fernandel), a hunchback who works in a Marseilles brick factory is in love with Naïs (Jacqueline), daughter of Micoulin the farmer. But Naïs secretly loves Frédéric Rostaing, the factory owner's son. Frédéric is a law student but shows little interest in his studies to which he prefers gambling and chasing women. One day Micoulin stumbles upon Naïs in the arms of her lover and goes into a rage and during the next few days attempts to shoot Frédéric several times but fortunately he fails. Naïs is worried and asks Toine for help. In the meantime, Micoulin has placed dynamite near a fishing hole frequented by Frédéric but Toine lights up the wick and kills Micoulin. Frédéric then leaves for Paris to pursue his studies and Naïs, expecting child, promises to marry Toine.

In September 1946, Raimu died in the American Hospital of Neuilly. The same month Pagnol was elected at the French Academy thanks to his friends Pierre Benoit and François Mauriac. Unlike Mistral and Daudet, Pagnol enjoyed clubs and honors and was proud of being a member of the distinguished institution. "I find our Thursday meetings quite pleasant and very interesting. There I meet famous scholars, dukes, philosophers, scientists, doctors, and novelists who speak like everybody else," he told Norbert Calmels.[18] From 1947 to 1951, the Pagnols resided in Monaco where they took an active part in the social and artistic events in the company of young Prince Rainier. Pagnol gave himself a break from Provençal themes and wrote a French version of A *Midsummer Night's Dream* and of *Hamlet,* directed by Serge Reggiani and performed at the Angers Summer Festival in 1955. In 1948, Pagnol directed a film, *La Belle Meunière,* inspired by the life of musician Franz Schubert. Jacqueline and Corsican singer Tino Rossi starred in the leading roles and it was Pagnol's first color film but the subject failed to interest the public with a color system invented by the brothers Roux. The film failed. In 1951, Pagnol's father died in Marseilles where he had finished his career as a school principal.

In 1952, the Pagnols were back in Paris but Pagnol was mostly in La Treille to shoot his masterpiece *Manon des Sources.* His production team had now been working together for over twenty years and the cast

included regulars such as Poupon, Blavette, Rellys (Ugolin), Jacqueline (Manon) and Raymond Pellegrin (the young teacher). The original version lasted three hours and only alluded to the previous story, which was later developed into a film and called first *Ugolin* and then *Jean de Florette*. Jean, his wife and daughter Manon, leave Paris to settle in Provence on a farm he inherited from his late mother, Florette. Jean, a hunchback, is an engineer who has decided to go back to nature and live off the land. But Papet, an old peasant and Ugolin, his last relative do not like Jean and see him as a competitor. The major problem for agriculture in the area is the lack of water. Jean does not know that there is a hidden spring on his land and before he finds out, Papet and Ugolin block it. In the meantime, Jean digs a well with dynamite and unfortunately is killed by a falling rock. His wife and daughter leave but shortly before their departure Manon sees Papet and Ugolin unplug the spring and dance frantically with joy. She is horrified but keeps the secret.

Manon des Sources begins ten years later when Manon, now a young woman, returns to her father's property and discovers a higher spring in the mountain which she blocks and thus deprives the entire village of water. The population is worried, engineers and geologists are brought to he area, the priest invokes the wrath of God as punishment but finally Manon publicly accuses Ugolin and Papet. Ashamed, Ugolin, secretly in love with Manon, hangs himself. Later Papet learns a terrible secret…and patiently awaits death. These films remain, along with *Marius,* Pagnol's masterpieces. They were written into a novel and published in 1962 as *L'Eau des Collines*.

In 1955, Pagnol went back to the stage with *Judas*. The play, directed by Elvire Popesco and Hubert de Malet, premiered at the Théâtre de Paris on October 6, 1955 with Raymond Pellegrin in the role of Judas, Claude Brasseur and Jean Servais. The character of Judas had fascinated Pagnol for quite some time and particularly he fact that Jesus knew about his plan. His play emphasized the problematic aspects of the story as told in the New Testament. Critics applauded but on the twelfth performance Pellegrin fainted and his replacement was stricken with appendicitis on his second night, and the play stopped. Pagnol was not discouraged and the following year he created *Fabien*. Performed for the first time at the Théâtre des Bouffes-Parisiens, *Fabien* is the story of a young photographer (Philippe Nicaud) and his thirty-three year old and overweight wife Milly (Milly Mathis), whose marital life is temporarily shattered by the arrival of Marinette, Milly's younger sister

with whom Fabien falls in love. The play was a flop and stopped after a hundred performances. Pagnol and his friends could not understand the reason of his failed return to the stage but later realized that Fabien, a liar who cheats on his wife and produced pornography for the Germans during the war, was perhaps too despicable a character. Pagnol had certainly done better and the public was rightly disappointed.

Pagnol was now busy writing his memoirs, *La Gloire de mon Père* and *Le Château de ma Mère,* recently successfully brought to the screen. In 1959 they were followed by *Le Temps des Secrets.* After a brief interruption, during which he translated Virgil's *Bucolica* (1959) and met with the young generation of movie makers such as François Truffaut and Claude Chabrol, Pagnol turned his interest to the television for which he gave numerous interviews, presided the international festivals in Monte Carlo, adapted *La Dame au Camelia* (1962) of Alexandre Dumas and his own *Merlusse* (1965). In his last years, he attempted, in his turn, to solve the famous mystery of the Man in the Iron Mask with his *L'Homme au Masque de Fer* (1973). Pagnol died in Paris on April 18, 1974. He was buried in La Treille.

Endnotes

1. "Il avait un extraordinaire don de conteur. Il le savait. Il s'en servait avec une virtuosité exceptionnelle." Raymond Castans, *Marcel Pagnol m'a raconté* (Paris: Editions de la Table Ronde, 1975) 20.
2. "Je suis né dans la ville d'Aubagne, sous le Garlaban couronné de chèvres, au temps des derniers chevriers." *La Gloire de Mon Père: Souvenirs d'Enfance* (Paris: Editions de Fallois, 1988) 11. "Je vins au monde au pied d'un figuier, il y a vingt-cinq ans, un jour que les cigales chantaient et que les figues-fleurs, distillant leur goutte de miel, s'ouvraient au soleil et faisaient la perle." Paul Arène, *Jean des Figues* (Raphèle-les-Arles: Marcel Petit, 1979) 3.
3. "Nichée sur les coteaux de la vallée de l'Huveaune et traversée par la route poudreuse qui allait de Marseille à Toulon. On y cuisait de tuiles, des briques et des cruches, on y bourrait des boudins et des andouilles…" Pagnol 21.
4. "Un incendie en plein jour." André Suarès, *Marsiho* (Paris: Grasset, 1933) 9.
5. "Il ne faut jamais oublier la Grèce, si l'on veut comprendre le fond du pays." Suarès 88.
6. Edouard Baratier ed. *Histoire de Marseille* (Toulouse: Privat, 1987) 367.
7. Baratier 385.
8. "La vie des collines." Jacques Bens, *Pagnol* (Paris: Seuil, 1994) 28.
9. "Paris, que j'imaginais comme une fourmilière sous la pluie, me faisait peur." Pagnol, *Confidences* (Paris: de Fallois, 1990) 10.

10. C.E.J. Caldicott, *Marcel Pagnol* (Boston: Twayne Publishers, 1977) 50.

11. "J'ai entendu dans l'ombre les applaudissements de Molière et de Marivaux." *Album Pagnol* (Paris: de Fallois, 1993) 48.

12. "Je voyais dans mes rêves le peuple joyeux des pêcheurs et des poissonnières...je retrouvais l'odeur des profonds magasins où l'on voit dans l'ombre des rouleaux de cordages, des voiles pliées sur des étagères et de grosses lanternes de cuivre suspendues au plafond, je revis les petits bars ombreux le long des quais et les fraîches Marseillaises aux éventaires de coquillages. Alors avec beaucoup d'amitié je commençais à écrire l'histoire de ce Marius..." Jean-Paul Cléber, *La Provence de Pagnol* (Aix-en-Provence: Edisud, 1986) 49.

13. "Tu devrais écrire une pièce marseillaise, qui se passerait sur le Vieux Port." Pagnol, *Confidences* 96.

14. "Il éclata comme une bombe. Le film tint l'affiche pendant vingt-cinq semaines consécutives." Pagnol, *Cinématurgie de Paris* (Monaco: Pastorelly, 1980) 50.

15. "Le cinéma c'est désormais l'affaire des auteurs dramatiques...être muet c'est une infirmité comme être boiteux....C'est un art nouveau qui vient de naître. Je n'écrirai plus de pièces de théâtre. J'écrirai des films." *Album Pagnol* 59.

16. "J'étais assez surpris de retrouver chaque jour dans le restaurant des studios trois César, trois Fanny, trois Marius, trois Escartefique qui étaient incapables d'échanger deux mots entre eux sauf..." Pagnol, *Cinématurgie de Paris* 58.

17. Raymond Castans, *Marcel Pagnol: Biographie* (Paris: Lattès, 1987) 193.

18. "Je trouve très agréable et fort intéressant d'assister à nos réunions du jeudi. J'y rencontre des savants célèbres, des ducs, des philosophes, des scientifiques, des médecins, des romanciers qui parlent comme tout le monde." Norbert Calmels, *Rencontres avec Marcel Pagnol* (Monaco: Editions Pastorelly, 1978) 142.

Six

Jean Giono

Jean Giono was born in the town of Manosque on March 3, 1895. His paternal grandfather Pietro Antonio had left his native Piedmont in the 1840s to settle in Provence. There, he held various occupations, probably worked as a minor and may also have taken part in the construction of a dam near Aix-en-Provence under the direction of engineer Zola, father of the novelist, who also came from Piedmont. Pietro lived in the village of Saint-Chamas on the banks of the Berre Lake and married Angela Maria Astegniano, of Italian descent. The couple had four children among whom Jean Antoine, Giono's father. When Jean Antoine was nine years old, in 1854, Pietro passed away and the family moved to Peyrolles where their mother Maria managed an inn. As a young man, Jean Antoine worked for some time in Marseilles where he lived with his sister, but, after the death of his mother in 1874, he returned to Piedmont. Information about his whereabouts there is scanty. However, in 1883, he came back to Provence through the Alps, worked

Jean Giono 1895–1970 (Photograph Amis de Jean Giono, Manosque).

in various mountain villages and finally, around 1891, made his home in the small town of Manosque.

A cobbler by trade, Jean Antoine was in his mid-forties and eager to start a family of his own when, in 1892, he married Pauline Pourcin, a local woman. Cyrille, her father, was a native of Manosque. Trained as a tanner, in 1850, Cyrille Pourcin began an army career that lasted nearly sixteen years and then took him to Crimea and Italy. In 1866, he retired in Paris and married his concubine Eugénie Lefebvre, a native of Picardie, who had already given him two daughters, Pauline and Hélène. The Pourcins lived in Paris until 1870 when, fleeing the Prussian invasion, they settled in Manosque. Giono had a great respect for his father. "I admired him. He was a sort of golden-eyed God with the beard of a good-natured Santa Claus," he later remarked.[1] Jean Antoine spoke a Piedmontese dialect, but he also knew Provençal and French. Those who knew him describe him as an independent thinker, anticlerical but very generous, one of the few men, who, when a cholera epidemic struck Manosque, went out of his way to help the sick and the dying. Compassion and a wandering life are two characteristics of Giono's protagonists. Giono also attributed his inclination for reverie to his father.[2]

Jean Giono spent his childhood at 14 Rue Grande, Manosque's main street, in an old and dark house without electricity or heating. He remembers that the roof leaked over his parents' bed and, that, on stormy nights, he could hear his father complain that it was raining on his beard! But rent was cheap and, to young Giono, the long, narrow corridors and dilapidated bedrooms resounded with "fantastic echoes and divine

murmurs."[3] Manosque, sixty miles north of Marseilles, situated on the
banks of the Durance, was then a sleepy little town of some four thousand people. In this alluvial plain, the soil was fertile and farmers grew
cereals, vegetables, fruit, and raised sheep. A coal mine was the only
industrial activity. Manosque was also a place where Provençal culture
was very much alive. Its residents expressed themselves in the vernacular, and together happily celebrated the festivals of San Brancai, Cara-
mantran, Chandeleur, Saint Aloi, and at Christmas time the *Pastorale.*
Men's favorite pastimes were *boules,* cards, and the yearly horse fair
that assembled not only Manosquins but also peasants from the neighboring villages perched on the desolate high plateaus.

Giono was first sent to the school Présentines de Saint-Charles and
in 1902 to the *collège.* Besides the regular subjects, he also studied some
English and Italian. He even went to catechism and took his commu-
nion. On the whole, he was a fairly good student. Manosquins were
lucky because the local authorities had made public secondary education there free long before it became a national law in 1931. But Giono's
only ambition, as he has often said, was to follow in his father's footsteps and become a cobbler. So, at the age of sixteen he stopped attend-
ing school. He was also eager to contribute to the family's income and,
in October 1911, he got his first job in a local bank with a starting salary
of thirty francs a month.

On Sundays, Giono would often go with his parents for walks in
the countryside during which he and his father would plant acorns.
Sometimes, he would accompany his family to Marseilles to visit his
aunt and cousins. There, his father would take him to the Plaine-Saint-
Michel, a park where young Pagnol, the same age, used to play. It is
possible that the two writers saw each other there for the first time. For
the holidays, Giono usually remained at home or would occasionally
visit relatives in Vallorbe (Switzerland), where another of his father's
sisters resided. Already as a child Giono showed signs of being a
dreamer, a *pantaiaire,* as his father used to call him in Provençal. He
preferred long walks in the country to sports. Later he will explain: "I
always hated crowds. I love deserts."[4] Alone in his room or in the town
library, Giono spent long hours reading French and foreign literature:
Lamartine, Sue, Dumas, Verne, but also Fenimore Cooper, Scott, Dickens, Defoe, Cervantes, Goethe, Dante and the Greek tragedians. However, his favorite author was Virgil, whom Mistral, Bosco, and Pagnol
admired as well. Since Giono was now earning his own money, he could
afford to buy books, and reading became a favorite pastime.

Giono was of a more robust physical condition than Pagnol and when the Great War began, in 1914, he was drafted and, after a few months' training in the Alps, was subsequently sent to the front in Alsace-Lorraine. Over the next three years, Giono fought in the trenches of Champagne, Flanders and the Vosges regions. He was once shell shocked and slightly injured, and like all soldiers, experienced the horrors and hardships of war, which marked him for life. Giono wrote cards and letters to his parents always reassuring them that the situation was not as bad as they imagined and, during long furloughs, he would travel back to Manosque and visit them. War did not stop his passion for literature and whenever he had a couple of hours Giono plunged into a book: Balzac, Stendhal, or Hugo. Between March 1915 and October 1916, he wrote five poems that were published in *La Dépêche des Alpes*.[5] Giono managed to come out of the war unscathed and, dismissed in October 1919, went straight back home. But war had a profound and lasting effect on Giono's life and conception of art. "I cannot forget war. I've been trying for twenty years, despite life, pains and joys, I could not wash war away" he wrote in 1937.[6] Like many of his compatriots, he felt disillusioned with man and politics and turned into a pacifist. Soon he began to think of celebrating life in all its force and beauty.

After working six months in a bank in Marseilles, Giono finally got his old job back in Manosque. At last he was home. Life slowly resumed its peaceful course of card games at the local café, copious family meals, and Sunday outings. Giono renewed acquaintance with his old friends but, more importantly, he began to seriously court Elise Maurin, a local girl whom he had met before the war. Unfortunately, in the middle of his romance, in April 1920, his father passed away. Mr. Giono had been ill for some time and his death was deeply mourned by his family and friends. According to his last wish, he was given a Protestant burial. The following June, Giono and Elise got married. He was twenty-five years old. Since neither Giono nor Elise was particularly religious they only had civil ceremony. Like Giono, Elise was an only child, two years younger, and, like him also, she came from a modest family. Her father, "a little happy go lucky sort of man, always with a smile and ready for a good joke," was a barber.[7] However, she had more schooling than Giono, obtained her *baccalauréat* in Aix and taught in Corsica for a year. The couple had little money and so Elise took up a job as an accountant to a wine merchant.

On Sundays they would go to the cinema or entertain both of their

families in their small apartment. Sometimes, he and Elise would simply stay at home, sit in their armchairs and watch the reflection of the sunset on Manosque's red-tiled roofs, moments which helped crystallize Giono's artistic genius. "There" he later explained, "and in all those winter Sunday afternoons spent face to face with the wonderful crimson tiles under the rain, I found most of the material for my novels."[8] Giono's work in the bank and his new life as a married man did not suppress in any way his insatiable appetite for literature and he continued to read avidly French but also German, Italian and Japanese authors.

Giono's first attempts at writing go back to his school days. At the time he wrote mainly poems but also started two novels. War did not deter his literary ambition for during his four years as a soldier he continued to pour forth poetry, and by the time he was back in Manosque, his passion for writing was already deeply rooted. "Neither my small town, nor my job, which I liked, could stop me from writing."[9] Between 1921 and 1924, several of his prose poems appeared in various local magazines such *La Criée* and *Les Cahiers de L'Artisan,* the latter edited by Lucien Jacques who soon became Giono's best friend. Jacques, four years older than Giono, had left Paris to make his home in Provence in 1921. He was a sculptor but his interests extended to poetry, dance, and music, and had some connections in the artistic world. He introduced Giono to more established writers such as Maxime Girieud and encouraged him to pursue his writing. Soon Giono and Jacques became good friends. The two men had indeed many affinities. They had a common aversion for war, political organizations, and academic art in general, but, unlike Giono, Jacques, a couple of years older, had contacts in literary circles. It is through Jacques also that Giono discovered Henri Fournier's *Le Grand Meaulnes,* soon after their first meeting in 1924. The following year, Giono was promoted in the bank and he and Elise moved to a bigger apartment in the same street where he lived as a child. It is there that, in 1926, Aline, his first daughter, was born.

Giono was now immersed in Homer and, inspired by the tales of "the divine liar" Odysseus, he began writing his own version of the Greek epic, which he entitled *Naissance de l'Odyssée.* In the first draft of his version of the Greek epic, Giono made use of Provençal and local idioms, but according to his biographer Pierre Citron, Jacques advised against it and before sending his manuscript to publisher Bernard Grasset, Giono diligently deleted them. Giono also had other interests and wrote a short notice on Elémir Bourges, a novelist from the small village of Pierrevert, near Manosque. However, it was during a visit to

Elise's cousins in the high and deserted plateaus of the Drôme region north of Manosque, that Giono found his inspiration. " Mountains are my mothers. I hate the ocean, I loathe it … the sight of glaciers and wild goat grazing grounds is enough to fire up my respiration and my blood," he later claimed.[10] In the meantime Grasset rejected *Naissance de l'Odyssée,* but having detected an undeniable talent, requested another novel. So Giono took up his pen and wrote *Colline* in three months. Jean Guéhenno, reader for Grasset, loved it as well as André Gide at Gallimard. Grasset sent Giono a contract for *Colline* and his next two novels. Gallimard offered him a contract for the next three. Following the publication of his book in February 1929, Giono traveled to Paris where he was introduced to Gide, Guéhenno, André Chamson, Jean Paulhan, Pierre Mac Orlan, and Léon-Paul Farge. But like Mistral, Giono never felt comfortable in the capital and, although proud of having been acclaimed by literary authorities, after ten days, he was glad to be back in Manosque.

Critics unanimously declared *Colline* a wonderful book. The story is set in hills of Haute Provence in the small village of Bastides where, despite the massive exodus to the valley, four families still cling to their rustic way of life. Life in the small community is hard but simple and people are happy. However, one day, strange things happen. The spring suddenly dries up, then young Marie is taken ill and finally a fire devastates the village, killing Gagou, a retarded waif adopted by the residents. The bewildered people suspect old Janet, the seer, to have put a curse on them and, after a long deliberation, decide to kill him. But before they can carry out their plan old Janet dies of natural causes and, as if their premonitions were right, almost immediately after his death, life resumes its normal course. The fire dies out and the spring flows again.

Colline is a powerful story and contains all the major themes that Giono later developed. At the root of Giono's thought is his belief in an all powerful and independent nature. Nature is seen as a process, as something alive and endowed with a soul. Fundamental to his early novels is this life force whose laws baffle most men. Giono saw in material progress a great enemy and fought against those who wanted to master and control nature. In the 1930s, he became the apostle of what is now called "Ecology" and argued that man must respect nature and live in harmony with it: "Rivers and springs are characters: they love, betray, lie, forests breathe…all that constitutes a society of living beings."[11] Others before him, such as Mistral and Daudet had certainly

poeticized nature, but Giono also gave it a philosophical dimension. In the high and barren plateaus above Manosque he had discovered its secrets. The land he describes is far from the clichés generally attributed to Provence. It is no longer a happy and fragrant country where rabbits hop among thyme and rosemary bushes, but a hard and dry land battered by cold winter winds and with hot summer months during which run rivers dry and cause crops to fail. Unlike in the valleys of lower Provence, where men have, to some extent, domesticated nature, these high plateaus remain wild and to translate this wilderness Giono uses powerful sensual images. He speaks of the flesh and blood of the earth, describes the various fragrances of trees and plants and manages to put into words its magical powers. The woods "dance," fountains "sing" and trees "speak softly."

But Giono was not Bernadin de Saint-Pierre, and *Colline* is also about the relationship of men and nature. Nature is seen as mysterious but not impenetrable and those who deign listen to her, like old Janet, can learn its inner workings. Such men are not scientists whose research and experiments serve to exploit nature, but seers and poets who understand and respect her almost intuitively. Hence behind Giono's poetic descriptions lies a moral imperative. Like a Taoist master, old Janet explains to Gondran, his son-in-law, that men are blind to the true order of things because instead of trying to understand it they only seek to control and exploit it. Therefore, ignorance as well as greed is the cause of all evil:

> You want to know what to do, but you don't even know the world you live in. You are aware that something is against you but you don't know what. All that because you looked around you without understanding. I bet you never thought of the Great Force? The Great Force of animals, plants and stones. The earth is not made for you, alone, for you to use.[12]

Man's relationship to nature is primordial and, as Giono argues, determines all social behavior. "One cannot isolate man. He is never alone. The face of the earth is in his heart."[13] Giono's next novel *Un de Baumugnes* (1929) continues the saga of these highlanders and offers Giono once more the chance to express his love of such forlorn and rugged mountains. "The real truth," declares Amédée, the young protagonist without any hesitation, " is that I am from this soil…it is this soil that made me…and shaped my thoughts, and I am proud of it."[14]

The story begins in a café, down in the valley. Amédée who comes in for a drink, notices, sitting in a corner, a melancholy looking fellow and, being naturally kind-hearted, begins to talk to him. Albin tells of his sorrows and explains that he is in love with Angèle, a farm girl who had left her parents' farm in the mountains the year before to follow Louis, her lover, to Marseilles, where she has been promised work. There Angèle finds herself with child and realizes that she misjudged Louis who, in fact, expected her to work for him as a prostitute. Amédée is moved by Albin's story and decides to help him out. So he travels to the hills and manages to find a job as a farm hand for Angèle's parents.

Soon Amédée suspects that someone is hidden in the cellar and, after a discreet investigation, discovers that the mysterious person is, in fact, Angèle with her baby son Pancrate. Angèle has finally escaped her ordeal in Marseilles and returned home but, shameful and afraid, she prefers to keep a low profile and is hiding in the cellar. Alerted by Amédée, Albin comes to rescue her and marries her. *Un de Baumugnes* is a beautiful love story, but it is also about true compassion and friendship for it also focuses on the character of Albin, the nomadic poet with a good heart, who helps his fellow-beings in a totally disinterested way. The novel was a success but as the younger Manosquin author Pierre Magnan recalls, prostitution and illegitimate children were taboo topics in town and his mother forbade him to read it.

Giono's third novel *Regain* (1930) completes what has been called Pan's trilogy. It takes place in the imaginary village of Aubignane in the middle of the rural exodus around the turn of the century. In his turn, Gaubert, the old blacksmith gets ready to go to town and leave behind Panturle, a sturdy bachelor in his forties and Mamèche. Mamèche has not been very fortunate. First her young son died a few years before after accidentally eating some hemlock, then her husband was buried alive when the well he was digging suddenly collapsed on him. Nevertheless, she is determined to prevent the village from dying out and intends to find Panturle a female companion. After several weeks of searching around the village she finally manages to lure into the area a knife sharpener and his fiancée Arsule. Mamèche's plan works as expected and soon Arsule falls in love with Panturle and abandons her companion. The new couple is determined to succeed and, combining their efforts, begin to till the land.

After months, their labor finally pays off and farmers not only rush to buy their beautiful wheat but also begin to settle in the village and follow in their footsteps. Soon another couple with children moves into

the area and before long Arsule herself becomes pregnant. The village springs back to life. *Regain* is a hymn to rustic life but Giono also argues that such life is not for everybody and especially not for intellectuals. To illustrate his point the book also contains the unhappy adventure of a professor from the city who attempts to return to nature. Despite all his scientific knowledge, he fails to raise crops and finally returns to the city, an anecdote which, incidentally, Pagnol must have remembered when he wrote *Jean de Florette*.

At the same time as he was slowly becoming the prophet of a younger generation dissatisfied with urban life and materialism, Giono, in turn, discovered new writers. First, Walt Whitman in whom he found a kindred soul. Whitman's *Leaves of Grass* gave him "un inégalable bonheur" and opened new horizons, "un monde nouveau à nul autre pareil."[15] During the early 1930s, Giono was equally fascinated with Thomas Hardy's novels such as *Jude the Obscure* and *The Mayor of Casterbridge*. Later, he turned to Melville and Faulkner with whom he often liked to compare himself for, according to him, his Provence, like Faulkner's South, was an invention of his own. Giono reacted virulently against critics who saw in him another regional writer of the bucolic realism genre. He insisted that his art had nothing to do with realism. Art, truly understood, was necessarily subjective Giono argued, and the artist "painter of his time" was only an illusion.[16] "Reality," he often said, was "of no interest"[17] to him, except in as much as it mirrored itself in his mind, a more complex fact and conception that he shared with Stendhal.[18] Jean-Marie Le Clézio is perhaps not far from the truth when he says that Giono "discovers reality" and that "without ever losing sight of it, represents it as his invention."[19] On the whole, like Bosco, Giono considered himself more as a poet rather than as novelist. But as he explained in an interview with Jean Carrière, in his mind, true poetry was the art of life and, as such, went beyond writing: "It is an art that need not be written...great poets are those who enjoy life, those who put their poetry into the lives they lead."[20] Like Bosco and Pagnol, Giono also used the term "conteur" (storyteller) to describe his art. In any case, imagination was for him the essential quality of the artist and, as he has often declared: "The important thing is to be subjective."[21]

But Giono is a complex writer and although he is invariably a child of Provence, unlike Bosco and Pagnol, he always refused to be categorized as a local-color writer. The latter label has, it is true, a tendency to belittle and reduce the dimension and depth of his art and we can easily sympathize and understand Giono's reaction. When interviewed on

his relationship to "Provence" Giono was generally negative, claiming at times, that he had no ties with it whatsoever and that the best writer who described Provence was Shakespeare! "I do not know Provence. When I hear of this country, I promise myself never to set foot in it," he jotted down in his *Journal* in 1936, as if he wanted to oppose himself to Pagnol, the other young and successful author who, unlike him and in his own way, had taken the cause of Provence.[22] Historical circumstances can also account for Giono's attitude toward the South, for in his day, what was generally understood by Provence was a world delimited by the Papal Palace of Avignon and the casinos of the Riviera which, according to Giono, was made up of papier maché for the sole enjoyment of a rich cultured class in search of exoticism. Such was not the Provence he knew, and the merit of his novels is, to have stayed away from the usual clichés to reveal to the great public a darker and more secret country.

Giono's attitude vis-à-vis Provence, often misunderstood, inevitably became suspicious to his contemporaries. Bosco himself found Giono's aloofness somewhat reprehensible. "One day he denied being Provençal, it was a mistake and I was hurt." According to Bosco, Giono was deluded when he maintained that he had no ties to Provence: "When you consider how deeply indebted he is to his birthplace, I think it is almost impossible to separate the one from the other, despite what he says. No one, not even Giono himself, could separate such a son from such a mother."[23] Giono had read Bosco and first paid him a visit in Lourmarin on a hot summer day in 1929. The two writers conversed amicably all afternoon, but there were very few affinities between them, or so it seemed then to Bosco, and they did not see very much of each other in the next decades. According to Bosco, Giono was a man of higher Provence and as such belonged to a slightly different sensibility for, up there, as opposed to in the Rhône valley, things are different: "The expression of the eyes, the direction and the fullness of winds, thought processes, without presenting sharp contrasts, follow their inclinations and are subject to magnetisms."[24] Bosco may have exaggerated the contrast, but nevertheless his remarks on higher Provence are interesting and explain in part why Giono did not recognize himself in the land of Mistral and Daudet. But historical circumstances also play a role in Giono's case for to those like himself who had fought in the trenches of the World War I the defense of Provence seemed inconsequential. What mattered then and to his eyes was to show how peace and harmony were still possible. In his opinion, the ideal of the *Félibres* belonged to the romantic past, forever shattered by the war.

But Bosco clearly saw that Giono could hardly be separated from Provence, which like Faulkner's South, unconsciously fashioned his imagination and language, and furnished him with material for his stories in a way which invariably draws him closer to Pagnol than to Flaubert or Proust. As Manosquin Lucien Bruno remarks: "There is no doubt that all the places that Giono describes so well in his books truly exist."[25] Likewise for novelist and friend Pierre Magnan, Giono is undeniably a man of Provence.[26] Giono was attached to his land which, save for a few short trips, he only reluctantly abandoned. "I will never leave this country," he once said speaking of his beloved high plateaus: "It gave me and still gives me, each day, everything that I love."[27] Despite what he said, Giono knew Provençal, without which he could not have understood the people of higher Provence for as Maurice Chevaly shows in his history of Manosque, the language remained widely used by the population until the end of World War II.[28] Giono himself confided that, in the spring of 1929, being a guest speaker of the village of Puymoisson, on the Valensole plateau, he told the story of *Colline* half in French half in Provençal.[29]

What awakened Giono's artistic sensibility was his discovery of the high and half-deserted plateaus above his hometown. As early as 1924, he wrote to Jacques:

> If you ever come by my house, and I hope you will, I'll show you a strange spectacle: a land of hills and plateaus where seven or eight small villages lie dormant completely deserted... grass grows in their small streets, their roofs sag, and nettles creep up against their low windows. An immense silence contains them, and I know nothing more terrifying than night descending on these abandoned homes. Dear friend, all the inhabitants of such villages have been swallowed up by Marseilles.[30]

Mysterious, tragic, and strange, these places looked to him as if they had "just emerged from the deluge"and represented a pristine and unspoilt Provence.[31] No one before him, he later claimed again, had ever spoken of these godforsaken lands.[32]

Giono was right and his first three novels soon brought him notoriety and international fame. Journalists and critics, including Gide, Darius Milhaud, Léon Paul Fargue, and Adrienne Monier, manager of the Odéon bookstore, flocked to Manosque to pay him a visit. Movie producers followed. Giono could never say no and his guests were

always welcome but, as the number of interviews increased, he soon found himself pressed for time for he was still a bank clerk and had not yet contemplated being a full-time writer. Elise helped her husband as best she could, entertaining their guests and typing letters, but fame began to take its toll and so in November 1929, after eighteen years of dutiful service, Giono resigned from his position in the bank. The Gionos moved then to the outskirts of town and bought a small house that they named in Provençal "Lou Paraïs" (Paradise). It was located on the slope of the Mont d'Or and Giono lived there with his family, his mother and her brother. All, friends and visitors, noted his affability and generosity and attested to his delight in telling stories. For him, as for Daudet, Bosco, and Pagnol, myth and reality were inextricably woven together.

Giono now turned to his own life for inspiration. *Jean le Bleu* (1931) is based on his childhood days in Manosque and pays a tribute to his father Jean Antoine. To the latter Giono owed a profound respect for craftsmanship, his defiance of religious dogmas, and his admiration for truly compassionate people. In this autobiographical story, Giono also evokes the singular characters who played an important role in his childhood such as the mysterious man in black with a deep voice who read the *Illiad* to him in the middle of a field, and Francesco Odripano, an older Italian who taught him the importance of detachment from material possessions and spoke of the happiness of the people of the high plateaus. Giono ended his memories on the eve of his departure for the Great War, which became the subject of his next novel *Le Grand Troupeau* (1931). This story acted as a catharsis, for it gave him the opportunity to tell all the horrors and absurdities of wars and to show the advantages of peaceful solutions. But denouncing war was not enough and Giono now wanted to develop his philosophy and so he turned for Provence to set his next story.

Le Chant du Monde (1934) takes us to the imaginary "pays Rebeillard," a wilderness area, hidden from civilization by mists and red pine hills and where foxes, hawks, hares and deer live in harmony with a handful of country people. Antonio, a sturdy man in his forties, lives alone on a small island in the middle of the river. Antonio is not an ordinary man and his prolonged contact with wild life has taught him all the secrets of nature. He knows its most intimate rhythms, can predict storms and floods, and catches fish with his bare hands. One day, his friend Matelot, who lives in the neighboring valley, comes to ask him to help investigate the mysterious disappearance of his son Danis during

a fishing excursion. While they search the river, Antonio and Matelot meet Clara, a blind woman ready to give birth and assist her through her suffering. After several days, the search for Danis proves inconclusive and the two men pay a visit to old Toussaint, in the village of Fontvieille. Toussaint informs them that Danis is alive but in serious trouble for, blinded by his love for Gina, the daughter of a powerful farmer and landowner named Maudru, he fought and killed Maudru's nephew in a duel and later eloped with Gina. As Antonio and Matelot proceed to rescue Danis and Gina, a ferocious battle breaks out during which Maudru's farm is burned down and Matelot stabbed to death. Fortunately Antonio, Gina, and Danis manage to leave unscathed. Finally, Antonio and Clara, now his companion, go back to the island on the river. Unlike his preceding novels, *Le Chant du Monde* is one of the few stories in which Giono introduces valley people and in which water plays a major role. It is, in this respect, very reminiscent of Bosco.

At *Lou Paraïs*, Giono, comfortably installed in the attic room, wrote prolifically. In 1932, he was contacted by Pagnol, who enjoyed his novels, and asked him for permission to adapt some of his stories for the screen. Giono agreed and promised to collaborate with him and between the two Provençals, a long friendship began. In the meantime, family life continued with its sorrows and joys and in 1934 the Gionos were proud to announce the birth of their second daughter Sylvie. The mid-thirties were also marked by his active militant activities. Giono joined the leftist AEAR (Association of Revolutionary Artists), participated in the fight against fascism, and became the leading advocate of the peace movement. He was fast becoming a veritable prophet for the young intellectuals and his next novel *Que ma Joie Demeure* (1935) generated an immense enthusiasm. He was however, not always at ease with intellectuals and always maintained some distance with leftist groups, particularly communists. "I belong to the people more than a radical professor," he wrote in his *Voyage en Italie*.[33]

Que ma Joie Demeure is certainly one of the best novels, if not the best, that Giono ever wrote during his early years and the message it contains is still powerful. The story takes the reader back to the hills above Manosque. Up near the Gremone Pass in the fictitious village of Roume live a handful of farmers who eke out a meager living. Bobi, a vagabond and sometime juggler, wanders one day through the plateau and asks farmer Jourdan and his wife Marthe for shelter. The vagabond and the lonely couple talk late into the night and Bobi's esoteric knowledge of nature and agriculture soon fascinate and intrigue Jourdan and

Marthe. During the next few days, the couple decides to put Bobi's ideas into practice. His philosophy, a mixture of ecology, agriculture and poetry, soon find listening ears among the neighboring peasant population who, following his advice, manage to bring wild life (deer) back into the area. Then, they set free a stallion and begin to decorate their houses with flowers. Slowly, Bobi becomes their *guru*. He teaches them the art of sharing, organizes picnics and festivals and his efforts finally bring back their lost communal spirit. Unfortunately, in this exuberant return of life lurks the ever-present shadow of death and, in the midst of all this happiness, young Aurore shoots herself in the mouth. After about two years, his mission accomplished, Bobi leaves the happy community, but as he walks through a forest, on a stormy day, he is mortally stricken by lightning.

Following the publication of the *Que ma Joie Demeure,* scores of young disciples, including many communists, from France but also from all over Europe came to Manosque to meet their new prophet. Giono had become their Bobi and he played the role with pride and enthusiasm. In the fall of 1935 in the hamlet of Contadour, at three thousand feet altitude and at about twenty-five miles north of Manosque, Giono led his first group of about fifty followers to a summer retreat. They met regularly twice a year, in the summer and at Easter, until World War II. Giono seems to have accepted his new role of leader willingly and, as the numbers of followers increased, he and some of his closest friends bought an old farm there and established a more permanent residence. The majority of the Contadourians were of writers and teachers, but there was also a handful of artisans from the region including Pierre Citron his future biographer, and Magnan. The happy Contadourians shared food and chores, some slept outdoors in tents, others inside the farm. Giono, according to Magnan, rented a room in a nearby farm. They built their own furniture, made goat cheese and bathed in the river, and at night, assembled around their prophet to discuss existence, love, art, and peace.

Giono's new role as a leader forced him to clarify some of his concepts, which he did in a series of essays and pamphlets such as *Les Vraies Richesses* (1936), where he further argues that man's estrangement from nature was caused by greed and developed by the Industrial Revolution which, far from liberating him, had turned him into a machine and alienated him from his fellow beings.[34] In *Le Triomphe de la Vie* (1942), Giono attempts to rehabilitate manual labor and craftsmanship in general and, taking his father as an example, explains in

detail the art of the cobbler. In the same work he continues to criticize the development of technology which he sees as an obstacle for life, he maintains, implies, in fact, is a movement backward into the past which itself gives it meaning: "Existence is a mandatory step backward, at every moment. Indeed, to live is to know the world, which means to remember."[35] Giono was not a Marxist but shared with Marx the romantic vision of a golden rustic age. Unlike Marx, however, he did not advocate social warfare. On the contrary, his solution, much more akin to that of American transcendalists, advocated slow and individual changes. His message remains above all moral and poetic.

In 1936, assisted by Jacques and Joan Smith, Giono undertook the translation of Herman Melville's *Moby Dick,* which occupied him for the next four years. He probably discovered Melville around 1930 through his friend Henri Fluchère, English teacher and translator of Shakespeare, who, realizing that the famous American novel had never found a French translator, immediately thought of Giono to accomplish the task. The resemblance between Giono and Melville is far from obvious but the struggle between man and a powerful beast seems to have fascinated the former as well as the solitude and determination of Captain Ahab. Giono carried *Moby Dick* with him everywhere he went, like a Bible.

> This book was my foreign companion. I'd always take it to my wanderings across the hills. So at the very moment when I often perused these great solitudes immobile yet undulating like the ocean, all I needed to do was to sit down my back against the trunk of a pine tree, and take out that book already lapping to feel underneath and around me the swelling of the many lives of the ocean.[36]

To some extent, Giono may have seen himself as a Provençal Ahab. "There are, in the midst of peace (and consequently in the very midst of war), formidable combats in which one alone is engaged and whose uproars remain silent to the rest of the world," he wrote in his tribute to Melville.[37]

The long and arduous translation of Melville did not stop Giono's creative energy nor did it interfere with his new interest in the cinema. In the summer of 1936, he traveled to Paris to meet Pagnol and work on the screen adaptation of *Regain.* Collaboration was, from the start, difficult and the two men rarely agreed, so that, after a few days, Giono left Pagnol in charge. But the misunderstanding was only short-lived

and the following October, Giono went to La Treille to help supervise the shooting of the film. Giono enjoyed his stay and struck up friendships with Pagnol's team but he was bothered by Pagnol's interpretation of his novel and by the necessary cuts and changes that the making of a movie required. In November, he was invited to Grenoble to preside over a congress of regional writers.

In the meantime, Giono was working on a new novel, *Bataille dans la Montagne,* published in 1937. The story is about a flood which occurs after a large pocket of water contained in a glacier accidentally burst and floods several villages in the valley (influence of *Moby Dick*?). Survivors are isolated and trapped, and the situation seems desperate until the arrival of an unusual character, Saint Jean. The latter, a carpenter by trade, comes to the rescue and begins by killing a huge bull gone mad who is terrifying the population. Then Saint Jean assembles able-bodied men and blows up the dam downstream to let the waters evacuate. Meanwhile, Saint Jean has falls in love with Sarah who lives with Boromé, the village elder. Boromé broke his leg in the flood and cannot part with Sarah so Saint Jean chooses to leave. Critics were divided and many reproached the novel for its length and its unhappy ending.

In 1936, Giono launched *Les Cahiers du Contadour,* a review that published articles by him and others such as Fluchère, Christian Michelfelder, and Girieud. Two years later, the number of subscribers reached 530 and the review, now published three times a year, included excerpts from his translation of *Moby Dick.* During the same period, passages from *Les Deux Cavaliers de l'Orage* were published as separate short stories between 1938 and 1942.[38] The story takes place in the quiet village of Lachau in a valley near Manosque, where, in the hot and dry summer afternoons, older women, comfortably installed in their wicker chairs, reminisce about the past under the sycamore trees. There, every year, farmers of the neighboring villages gather to attend the famous horse and peacock fair. It is also there that Marceau Jason a solid horse breeder, kills with his bare fists a horse gone mad who had trampled several people. A few weeks later, Clefs-de-Coeur, a professional wrestler, having heard of the prowess of this new Hercules, challenges him to a fight. The two compete against each other and finally Marceau wins. Realizing that he is uncommonly strong, Marceau goes from town to town and begins in his turn a series of tournaments during which he challenges all of the best wrestlers. In the meantime, Mon Cadet, Marceau's beloved younger brother, becomes jealous of Marceau's success and finally challenges him to a fight. At first Marceau does not take

his brother seriously but then, realizing his determination, accepts the challenge. Despite the odds, Mon Cadet wins. The end is tragic for, unable to accept his defeat, a few days later, Marceau kills his brother with a scythe.

As the threat of war became more ominous, Giono became more and more outspoken in his movement for peace and devoted several pieces of writing to the cause. "Refuse war. That is the decision I, finally, after a long reflection, have taken for several years and I will not budge; ever" he wrote down in his journal.[39] In a series of pamphlets such as *Refus d'Obéissance* (1837), Giono accused capitalists of fomenting the war and denounced the absurdity and futility of armed conflicts. In 1938, in *Poids du Ciel* and *Précisions,* he went even further and blamed war on social organizations in general for as he says: "In any circumstances, social life demands that society have power against nature and over man."[40] So, as a remedy against the evil consequences of man's innate gregariousness, Giono advocated solitude: "Truth is only found in solitude. All social systems are built on lies."[41] In his *Lettre aux Paysans,* published the same year, Giono presented farmers as a race and not a class and even spoke of a "civilisation paysanne." He also recalled, with a touch of romanticism, the time, not long gone, when peasants still living in harmony with nature were proud, free and happy. *Recherche de la Pureté* (1939) continued along the same lines. Giono relied on his own experience of the Great War to argue that war is unnatural to man and invented by corrupt governments: "People never desire war; war is always imposed. There are no warmonger countries: there are only warmonger governments."[42]

In the spring 1939, and upon the initiative of some of his friends, Giono formed the bold but quite serious plan of meeting with Hitler to discuss the possibility of peaceful solutions. The encounter between the poet and the Nazi never took place but nevertheless the whole affair shows that Giono was more determined than ever to do everything in his power to avoid spilling innocent blood. When war inevitably broke out a couple of months later, Giono refused to be drafted and, despite his age (45), was incarcerated in Marseilles. There from October to November 1939, he led the life of an inmate but never lost hope. Thanks to the help his friends, he was finally freed and discharged of his military duties. He then went back to Manosque and began writing *Pour Saluer Melville,* his own interpretation of the life and art of the American writer. The book was published in 1941. Life in France was taking a dramatic turn and the German occupation and the forced collaboration

caused the population to further suffer and divide. The Gionos were not spared and in order to compensate for the lack of food supplies, Giono bought two farms near Manosque, one at Céreste and the other at Mane. There, he managed to raise some cattle and grow plants to insure the subsistence of his family. Royalties from his publishers were hard to come by and Giono was often forced to write prefaces for books.

During the Occupation, disagreements with Pagnol grew worse and in 1941 ended up in court in Marseilles. Giono accused Pagnol of plagiarizing him especially in his new movie *La Femme du Boulanger* but he lost. Pagnol, who had obviously borrowed from Giono, was lucky. But Giono, in turn, was keeping a closer look on Pagnol's dramatic techniques and dreamed of taking his revenge with the same weapons. In fact as early as 1931, Giono had written a play *Le Bout de la Route* that was now being performed for the first time in Paris at the Théâtre des Noctambules (May 1941). His drama met with some success but could not compare with that of Pagnol. Then, Giono wrote his own stage version of *La Femme de Boulanger* (1944) but the play failed to arouse the interest of the public and the critics. In 1942, Giono spent a month in Paris to sign contracts with Grasset and renew acquaintance with some of the older writers still in the city such as Cocteau. Back in Manosque, Giono set to writing again but rheumatism in his right arm forced to hire a secretary, Alice Servin, and now took the habit of dictating his novels.

Real trouble began for Giono when both communists and pro-rightist governments, irked at his negative comments concerning their ideologies, blacklisted him. Things got worse yet with the publication of some passages of *Les Deux Cavaliers de l'Orage* and a photo of him in the pro-German magazine *La Gerbe*. Then, the situation rapidly deteriorated and accusations of collaboration with the enemy were made. In 1943, a bomb exploded in front of his home in Manosque. Fortunately the charge was small and the damage only material, but the following year Giono was again arrested and taken to jail, first in Digne, and then in Saint-Vincent-les-Forts. This time his incarceration lasted five long months, until the court, lacking evidence, finally agreed to release him, forbidding him to reside in his hometown. Giono and his family lived then with friends in Marseilles and Cassis until 1946 when they were finally allowed to return home. Rumors of his alleged collaboration with the Germans had had dramatic consequences and his books continued to be boycotted, but that did not stop Gallimard to publish *L'Eau Vive* (1943), a collection of his short stories previously published in magazines

such as *La Criée, Revue de Paris,* and *Nouvelle Revue Française* from 1930 to 1943.

War had again taken its toll and left Giono more disillusioned than ever. His artistic ideal took a sharp turn. Less idealistic and social in content the novels he now wrote reflected above all a preoccupation with style. He had recently rediscovered Stendhal, and Ariosto but was also reading American authors then in vogue such as Faulkner, Hemingway, Steinbeck and Dos Passos, and as a consequence Adensity replaced abundance,"as Citron correctly remarks.[43] Giono's style became subtler and in many ways anticipated or echoed the *Nouveau Roman.* However, considering the work as a whole, one realizes that it is not so much a change of form that takes place but rather a slow maturation. Giono was now a more mature and experienced writer.

Un Roi sans Divertissement (1947) is the first and perhaps the most successful novel of this period and one that certainly inspired younger writers such as Magnan. In 1843, high up in a forlorn plateau between Gap and Grenoble, some of the inhabitants of a small village mysteriously disappear one by one. One day twenty-year-old Marie Chazottes vanishes into thin air. Then, young Georges Ravanel is assaulted but miraculously rescued in time by his father. Identification of his assailant is unfortunately impossible, for the criminal has first thrown a bag over his victim's head. Nevertheless, this incident clarifies the case and it becomes obvious that those who have disappeared have been murdered. In the meantime, winter settles in and snow, as if to hush things up, falls heavily on the small village living in fear. Able-bodied men continue the search for Marie Chazottes but in vain. The plot thickens with the consecutive disappearance of two other villagers, Bergues the bachelor, and Dorothée. As the residents now begin to barricade themselves in their homes, one morning, Frédéric, a woodcutter, overhears a strange noise coming from an enormous beech tree and sees a shadow walking away from it. Acting with utmost precaution, Frédéric approaches the tree, looks up, but everything seems normal. Yet, to make sure he has not been tricked, he climbs the huge trunk and, with a horrifying surprise, discovers Dorotheé's body and the remains of the two others, hidden in the large cavity.

The woodcutter immediately follows the footprints on the snow, catches up with the shadow that was slowly making his way through the deep forest, and discreetly follows him all the way to a house in the village of Chichiliane. He then returns home, informs Langlois and the *gendarmes* who quickly organize a manhunt. The group stalk the

criminal, follow him out of his home and deep in the thick of the forest. Langlois confronts and then shoots him. However, the mystery remains and little is known about the criminal, his motive, and the reasons for his execution. Contrary to the reader's expectations, the novel is not finished. A few years later similar events occur, this time the criminal is a wolf and Langlois again shoots him in the same way he shot the first criminal. The novel as a whole is somewhat disconcerting but in the first part Giono showed that he also excelled in the detective genre. *Noé* (1948) is not a novel but rather an autobiographical story in which Giono talks about artistic techniques using anecdotes and mentioning specific events or people that inspired him.

Life at the Gionos' went on unchanged save for the departure of their daughter Aline for the University of Nice where she majored in English, and the arrival of Serafina Ughetto, a Piedmontese maid that Giono hired to help his wife with house chores. After months of arduous work in his attic room, Giono finished a new novel *Les Ames Fortes* (1950). The book was innovative and differed in style from his earlier writings. The narrator is absent and the characters express themselves as if they were on a stage. The narration is accomplished in turn by several characters that speak from various stages of their lives, a device that Giono used to show the different versions of the same story. The plot is basically rather simple. At the end the nineteenth century, Thérèse and Firmin work as maid and blacksmith for Mr. and Mrs. Numance, an older couple who, at the turn of the century, have retired in the small village near Châtillon in the rugged Drôme mountains, north of Manosque. Mrs. Numance loves Thérèse as the daughter she never had and even pays off Firmin's alleged debts. One day, however, we learn that Mr. Numance died and that his wife disappeared. Things are not so well either between Thérèse and Firmin who now begin to hate each other. Apparently, Thérèse has a lover and manages to cajole him into killing Firmin. Giono's novel certainly anticipated some of the techniques of the *Nouveau Roman* and was rather well received by the press.

But Giono did not persist in this direction and in his next novels returned to his favorite themes. *Les Grands Chemins* (1951) revolves around the fortuitous encounter between a hobo and "l'artiste," a young man and petty crook who earns his living cheating people at cards. The two become friends and travel through the small villages of northern Provence until one day "l'artiste," acting on his own, robs an old woman, kills her, and goes into hiding. The *gendarmes* later inform the young man that his friend is in fact a

dangerous ex-convict. Knowing his habits, the vagabond finds his companion before the police do and shoots him.

Le Hussard sur le Toit (1951) is often held as Giono's most successful novel of the later period. It takes place around 1820. Angelo Pardi, a twenty-six-year-old Italian officer of noble birth, escapes Piedmont after having killed a man in a duel and wanders about Provence. The country is unfortunately devastated by a terrible cholera epidemic that prevents Angelo from traveling freely and interferes with his search for his friend Giuseppe. Doing the best he can to avoid quarantine, Angelo meets hundreds of moribund and helps the sick and the dying. One day he finds love in the person of Pauline de Théus who miraculously survived the scourge. Finally, Angelo goes back to Italy. Reminiscent of Camus' *La Peste* (1947) in which an epidemic is also central to the story, Giono renews with the theme of death and the importance of caring but also shows man's failure to control and eradicate disease. The evil disappears the way it came. Suffering dominates the novel and is described in vivid details. Giono also takes the opportunity of showing how some men turn the epidemic into a successful moneymaking enterprise, selling carts, water or other necessities at a higher price.

A year after, Giono published *Le Moulin de Pologne* (1952), a novel that takes place in the mid-nineteenth century and addresses the problem of destiny. Giono tells the story of the Costes, a family strangely stricken with a series of inexplicable deaths. Mr. Coste and his two daughters leave Mexico where he had settled in the early days of the nineteenth century and return to his native Provence with the hope of changing the course of destiny. Sometime before his departure from Mexico, Coste's wife and his two sons died in accidents, one after the other. Coste is convinced that these deaths were not the result of unfortunate causes but on the contrary determined by fate. Hence he attempts to find his daughters Anaïs and Clara husbands from good and stable families that destiny has spared, and with the help of the local matchmaker Miss Hortense, narrows down his search to two rich farmers' sons who seem to meet the requirements. As Miss Hortense explains, nothing unusual has ever happened in their families even for many past generations. Coste is satisfied and begins preparations for the weddings. Anaïs marries Pierre and the couple settles in an old windmill. Soon she gives birth to a beautiful daughter Marie. Three years after, life seems to have resumed its normal course and Coste thinks he has finally managed to trick destiny.

However, one day his luck begins to change. At the age of three

Marie chokes on a cherry and dies, and on the same day her mother passes away giving birth to her son Jacques. From then on death takes over. Mr. Coste dies of tetanus a couple of days after he cuts his finger on a rusty fishhook. Clara, her husband Paul, and their two sons, who up to now have been spared, begin to fear for their lives and leave town. But they all meet their death when their train derails and crashes. Pierre, Anaïs's husband, seems to be spared, but depressed and without many prospects, he begins to drink and ends up in a lunatic asylum. Even Miss Hortense, who was not a member of the family, but who had played a major role in the weddings, one day falls down the stairs to her death. Jacques, the last descendant, marries Joséphine but dies of a heart attack at forty-two. His own children are also doomed. His son commits suicide and his daughter becomes shell-shocked after hearing gunfire.

The success of *Les Ames Fortes* and *Le Hussard sur le Toit* brought Giono back to the literary scene and slowly erased the dark episodes of the war. In 1952, he began a series of radio interviews with poet Jean Amrouche and later with Jacques Robichon. Once again, Giono was solicited for numerous prefaces. Reader's Digest approached him for a story but it is *Vogue* that finally printed *L'Homme qui plantait des Arbres*, a beautiful tale where poetry and ecology meet. Winning his public back, Giono became the recipient of numerous honors and prizes. In 1953, he received the Prix de Monaco. At this time André Maurois and Pagnol, with whom he had renewed friendship, pressured Giono to present his candidature to the French Academy but he instead opted for the Academy Goncourt where he was received in 1954, filling the seat left vacant by Colette's death.

Giono, who, except on rare occasions when he had to go to Paris, never left Provence, now began to travel. Italy, the land of his ancestors, was naturally first on the list and, in 1951, accompanied by his wife and a couple of friends he traveled there in a small Renault. The country charmed and fascinated him and he returned three times in 1957, 1958 and 1961. In 1952, Giono also visited Scotland and England where his daughter Aline was a French assistant at Chichester High School. Aline later became a teacher and then worked for Gallimard in Paris. In 1959, along with his wife Elise, Giono went to Spain and to the island of Majorca where, twice a year he would return. He also became interested in the cinema and wrote the scenario for *L'Eau Vive* (1958) starring Pascale Audret and Charles Blavette, and inspired by Pagnol, in 1959 he created his own film company "La société des films Jean Giono." He subsequently made *La Duchesse* (1959), a short film relating the

story of the Duchess of Berry, and then *Crésus* (1960) for which he hired a cast of Provençal actors including Marseillais Fernandel, Rellys and Paul Prébois.

The story takes place in 1947 on Giono's favorite high plateaus, above Banon. One day Jules (Fernandel) the shepherd finds a bomb filled with banknotes, over a billion Francs, and hides it in an empty water cistern. The joy of the first days is soon replaced by worry, and Jules consults the priest to make sure money is not sent by the devil. Reassured he then inquires into the possibility of investments, but finally decides to give a banquet and invite all of the villagers. The meal is paid in cash and prepared by a cook in Banon. Suspicion is de rigueur amongst the guests who all wonder where Jules, usually so poor like the rest of them, got the money. The situation becomes so tense that to calm them down Jules decides to give each of them a few banknotes. Jules continues his generous distribution everyday for a week but money changes the villagers' behavior who in their turn become worried, and afraid of being robbed, lose sleep and spy on each other until finally one day, they decide to ask Jules to stop.

In the meantime, two policemen, alerted by the cook from Banon, pay Jules a visit and explain to him that this money is counterfeit and was sent intentionally by the Americans to de-stabilize the economy. Everybody is happy to return the banknotes and to return to their simple existence and Jules proposes to Joséphine. The film is an allegory in which Giono shows all the problems that arise with money but humor and irony dominate in a well-written script, and definitely show the influence of Pagnol. Fernandel, who often acted for Pagnol, is more than at ease in a role almost cast for him. In 1961, Giono presided the Cannes Film Festival and, in 1963, he directed *Un Roi sans Divertissement* with actors Colette Renard and Charles Vanel. Cocteau seems to have been one of the rare critics who enjoyed the film. The same year Christian Marquand directed *Les Grands Chemins* featuring Robert Hossein.

Giono's love of Italy is reflected in the writings of this period. *Voyage en Italie* (1953) gives a personal account of his visit and *Le Désastre de Pavie* (1963) retraces the famous battle of 1525 when French king François I was defeated by Charles V of Spain. Italy is also present in his next novel *Le Bonheur Fou* (1957) which continues the adventures of Angelo Pardi during the Italian Resorgimento and in *Angelo* (1958), the unfinished sequel which tells about the protagonist's childhood and origins. In the late 1960s, Giono went back once more to his original

themes in a series of short tales such as *Le Déserteur* (1966), *Ennemonde et autres Caractères* (1968) and *L'Iris de Suze* (1970) which renew, one last time, with the world of vagabonds and shepherds of the high plateaus. Giono also worked on two other novels, *Olympe* and *Dragoon* which his death interrupted. Since the early 1960's, Giono's health, and especially his heart, had given him some trouble and he finally succumbed to a stroke at home on October 9, 1970. He is buried in Mansoque's cemetery.

Endnotes

1. "Je l'admirais, c'était une sorte de Dieu aux yeux dorés, à la barbe de Père Noël débonnaire." Jean Giono, *La Chasse au Bonheur* (Paris: Gallimard, 1928) 189.

2. "...la très grande habileté à rêver que je tiens de mon père." Giono, *Voyage en Italie* (Paris: Gallimard, 1954) 9.

3. "...des échos fantastiques et des chuchotements divins." Pierre Citron,*Giono* (Paris: Seuil, 1990) 34.

4. "J'ai toujours détesté la foule. J'aime les déserts..." Giono, *Voyage en Italie* 13.

5. Citron, *Giono* 83.

6. "Je ne peux pas oublier la guerre. Je le voudrais...depuis vingt ans. Malgré la vie, les douleurs et les bonheurs, je ne me suis pas lavé la guerre." Giono, *Refus d'Obéissance* (Paris: Gallimard, 1989) 261.

7. Citron, *Giono* 95.

8. "C'est de là, et de tous ces après-midi de dimanches d'hiver passés en tête-à-tête avec l'admirable pourpre des tuiles sous la pluie, que j'ai tiré une grande partie de mon fonds romanesque..." Citron 95.

9. "Ni la petite ville, ni mon métier auquel je m'intéressais, rien ne pouvait m'empêcher d'écrire." Citron 98.

10. "La montagne est ma mère. Je déteste la mer, j'en ai horreur...la vue des glaciers et des pâturages à chamois suffit à embraser ma respiration et mon sang." Giono, *Voyage en Italie* 12.

11. "Les rivières et les sources sont des personnages: elles aiment, elles trompent, elles mentent...les forêts respirent.... Tout cela est une société d'êtres vivants." Giono, *Solitude de la Pitié* (Paris: Gallimard, 1932) 148–49.

12. "Tu veux savoir ce qu'il faut faire, et tu ne connais pas seulement le monde où tu vis. Tu comprends que quelque chose est contre toi, et tu ne sais pas quoi. Tout ça parce que tu as regardé l'alentour sans te rendre compte. Je parie que tu n'as jamais pensé à la grande force? La grande force des bêtes, des plantes, et de la pierre. La terre c'est pas fait pour toi, unique, à ton usance..." Giono, *Colline* (Paris: Grasset, 1929) 111.

13. "On ne peut pas isoler l'homme. Il n'est pas isolé. Le visage de la terre est dans son coeur." Giono, *Solitude de la Pitié* 150.

14. "...dans le vrai fond, je suis de la terre...c'est cette terre qui m'a fait...moi, ma façon de penser, et j'en suis fier." Giono, *Un de Baumugnes* (Paris: Grasset, 1929) 43.

15. Pierre Citron ed. *Correspondance Jean Giono-Lucien Jacques*, 2 vols. (Paris: Gallimard, 1981) I: 133.

16. "L'artiste témoin de son temps est une invention, et pour le besoin d'une cause; il n'est que le témoin de lui-même." *De Homère à Machiavel, Cahiers Giono* (Paris: Gallimard, 1986) 15.

17. "La réalité est pour moi sans aucun intérêt." Jean Carrière, *Jean Giono: une Biographie et des Entretiens* (Besançon: Editions de la Manufacture, 1991) 126.

18. "Je me suis efforcé de décrire le monde, non pas comme il est mais comme il est quand je m'y ajoute, ce qui, évidemment ne le simplifie pas." Bosco, *Voyage en Italie* 57.

19. "Jean Giono découvre la réalité sans jamais la perdre de vue en nous la faisant voir comme irréelle." Jean-Marie Le Clézio, "Hommage à Jean Giono" *Le Figaro Littéraire* October 19–25, 1970, 14.

20. "C'est une fonction qui n'a pas besoin d'écriture...les grands poètes sont ceux qui jouissent de la vie, qui mettent leur poésie la vie qu'ils mènent." Carrière, *Jean Giono: une Biographie et des Entretiens* 126.

21. "L'important c'est d'être subjectif." Carrière 136.

22. "Je ne connais pas la Provence. Quand j'entends parler de ce pays, je me promets bien de n'y jamais mettre les pieds." Giono, *Journal* (Paris: Gallimard, 1995) 120.

23. "Il nia un jour d'être Provençal. C'était une erreur et j'en ai souffert. Quand on pense à tout ce qu'il doit à son pays natal, comment ne seraient-ils pas l'un à l'autre et, quoiqu'il en ait dit, inséparables? pas même Giono ne saurait désunir un tel fils d'une telle mère." Bosco, "Un poète de la lune et des astres" *Le Figaro Littéraire* October 19–25, 1970, 16.

24. "...le sens que prennent les regards, la direction, l'ampleur des souffles, le cheminement des pensées, sans s'opposer par vifs contrastes, obéissent à des attraits et subissent des magnétismes qui détachent insensiblement les deux pays et finissent par les distinguer." Bosco.

25. "Il n'y a pas de doute, que tous les lieux dont il parle dans ses livres, et qu'il sait si bien décrire, existent bien." Lucien Bruno, *Manosque au Temps Jadis* (Manosque: Rico, 1975) 92.

26. "Giono ne saurait être séparé de cette plaine de Manosque ...là est passé tout le charroi de son oeuvre et toutes ses passions." Pierre Magnan, *Pour Saluer Giono* (Paris: Denoel, 1990) 180

27. "Ce pays-ci, je ne le quitterai jamais. Il m'a donné, et il me donne encore chaque jour tout ce que j'aime." Giono, *Journal* 121.

28. Maurice Chevaly, *Giono à Manosque* (Saint-Maximin: Le Temps Parallèle, 1986) 54.

29. Citron ed. *Correspondance Jean Giono-Lucien Jacques* I:281.

30. "Si jamais vous venez par chez moi, ce que je souhaite, je vous montrerai une spectacle étrange: une région de collines et de plateaux où dorment

sept à huit petits villages absolument déserts…l'herbe poussent dans les ruelles, les toitures s'enfoncent, les orties fourrent les fenêtres basses. Un très grand silence les enferme et je ne sais rien de plus terrifiant que le soir descendant sur ces foyers perdus. Mon cher ami, tous les habitants de ces villages ont été mangés par Marseille." Citron 33.

31. "Un pays mystérieux, dramatique, étange, qui semble, à certains endroits…émerger à peine du déluge." Citron 80.

32. "On n'est jamais venu regarder la Provence d'ici." Giono, *L'Eau Vive* in *Oeuvres Romanesques Complètes* (Paris: Gallimard, 1974) III: 221.

33. "Je suis beaucoup plus du peuple qu'un agrégé d'extrême gauche." Giono, *Voyage en Italie* 158.

34. Giono, *Les Vraies Richesses* (Paris: Grasset, 1937) 18.

35. "Vivre est un obligatoire retour en arrière de chaque instant. En effet, vivre c'est connaître le monde, c'est à dire, se souvenir." Giono, *Triomphe de la Vie* (Paris: Grasset, 1982) 53.

36. "…ce livre a été mon compagnon étranger. Je l'emportais régulièrement avec moi dans mes courses à travers les collines. Ainsi, au moment même où souvent j'abordais ces grandes solitudes ondulées comme la mer mais immobiles, il me suffisait de m'asseoir, le dos contre le tronc d'un pin, de sortir de ma poche ce livre qui déjà clapotait pour sentir se gonfler sous moi et autour la vie multiple des mers." Giono, *Pour Saluer Melville* in *Oeuvres Romanesques Complètes* (Paris: Gallimard, 1974) 3.

37. "Il y a au milieu même de la paix (et par conséquent au milieu même de la guerre) de formidables combats dans lesquels on est seul engagé et dont le tumulte est silence pour le reste du monde." Giono 3.

38. Citron, *Giono* 536–37.

39. "Refus de guerre. C'est la résolution à laquelle je suis finalement, après mûre réflexion, arrêté depuis plusieurs années, et je n'en bougerai pas; jamais." Giono, *Journal* 110.

40. "La vie sociale quelle qu'elle soit, exige que la société possède une puissance contre nature sur l'homme." Giono, *Poids du Ciel* (Paris: Gallimard, 1989) 426.

41. "Il n'y a de vérité que dans la solitude. Tous les sytèmes sociaux ne sont que des constructions de mensonges." Giono.

42. "La guerre n'est jamais voulue par les peuples. Elle est toujours subie. Il n'y a pas de peuples guerriers; Il n'y a que des gouvernements guerriers." Giono, *Recherche de la Pureté* (Paris: Gallimard, 1989) 653.

43. "L'abondance va faire place à la densité." Citron, *Giono* 229.

Seven

Recent Writers

Encouraged by the example of Mistral and the *Félibres,* and keeping up the same tradition, many other writers continue to express themselves in Provençal. Marius Jouveau (1878–1949) was a prolific author and wrote primarily poetry and drama. Valère Bernard (1860–1936) was mainly a novelist (*Bagatouni,* 1894, *Lei Boumian* 1910) and short story writer. Many other names should also be mentioned such as Marcelle Drutel (*Li Desiranço* 1933, *De Souleu emai de Luno,* 1965), Fernand Moutet (*Fenestro,* 1962, *L'Autro Ribo,* 1969), Pierre Millet (*La Draio,* 1953, *La Sablo d'Angloro,* 1975), Jean Pierre Tennevin (*Lou Grand Baus,* 1965, *La Vieio qu'ero mouarto,* 1976), Max-Philippe Delavouet (*Pouemo,* 1983) and Bernat Gieli (*Flour de Camin* 1988, *L'Auro Fugidioso* 1990).

Other Provençal writers chose to write in French such as Sully André Peyre (1890–1961) whose poems echo Mistral and Louis Brauquier (1900–1976) who inspired Pagnol and Jean-Claude Izzo.

Louis Brauquier 1900–1976 (Photograph Editions Table Ronde, Paris).

Brauquier, a Marseillais, attended Lycée Thiers, shortly after Pagnol and then majored in law in Aix. Very early on, he discovered Emile Sicard, poet and editor of the review *Le Feu,* d'Arbaud and Blaise Cendrars, and his poetic vocation began. As a young man he created a review called *La Coupo* in which he wrote poems in Provençal but later switched to French. His collection of poems *Et L'au delà de Suez* received the Prix Catulle in 1923. The following year Brauquier became a *Commissaire de la marine marchande* and spent his life traveling around the world from Australia to Egypt and Ceylon, until he retired in 1960 in Saint-Mitre-les-Remparts, by the Etang de Berre. Two years later he received the Grand Prix Littéraire de Provence and in 1971 the French Academy awarded him the Grand Prix de Poésie.

    Brauquier was also a friend of Gabriel Audisio, Bosco and Pagnol who based the character of Marius on him. "*Marius* is *Et l'au-delà de Suez,* I owe you three million," Pagnol once told Brauquier.[1] His poems were published in collections such as *Le Bar de L'Escale* (1926), *Eau Douce pour navires* (1930) and *Liberté des Mers* (1940). Brauquier's favorite theme was the beauty of the sea and the world of sailors. He dedicated several poems to Marseilles, as "Nuits sur le Vieux Port" and "Litanies pour Notre-Dame de la Garde." Yvan

Audouard, a native of Arles, writes short novels in regional French (*Le Dernier des Camarguais* 1971, *Sarah des Sables* 1972, *Le Porte- plume* 1996) but particularly excels in the art of the tale like his predecessors Arène and Pagnol (*Contes de ma Provence,* 1986). Among contemporary novelists, three writers stand out, Marie Mauron, Pierre Magnan and Jean-Claude Izzo.

Marie Mauron was born in Saint-Rémy in 1896. Her parents Simon and Jeanne Roumanille (distant cousin of the poet) were farmers. The Roumanilles were not religious and politically belonged to the left. In 1898 her mother gave birth to a second child Maxime. Marie spent her childhood on the family *mas* and participated in all its activities: *olivades* or the gathering of olives in winter, and *vendanges* or grape picking in the fall. She also harvested and helped with the *décoconnage* of silkworms.

Marie first attended elementary school in Saint-Rémy and, her *certificat d'études* in hand four years later, she went to Beaucaire and then to Marseilles where she attended Mrs. Colombelle's class. Her teacher, Marcel Pagnol's aunt, would often take her students to the shore to collect plants and Pagnol, only one year older than Marie, would join them. Mrs. Colombelle would also collect some of her students' essays and publish them, with her nephew's approval, in his newly created review *Fortunio*.

The years 1913–1917 left a sad note in Mauron's memory for they corrrespond to the time she spent as a student at the *Ecole Normale* in Aix where she trained to be an elementary school teacher. Like her predecessors Mistral, Daudet and Bosco, Marie loved to roam freely the country and felt cooped up in the school. The strict discipline (she was grounded for reading Nietzsche) and her love of Mistral and Provençal poets were considered highly suspicious.[2] Fortunately Marie lived in town near the Méjanes library where she would immerse herself in books.

During the war, her mother, coming back one day from the fields with violent stomach pains, was taken care of by a young Alsatian doctor by the name of Albert Schweitzer. After graduation Marie was given a job first in Raphèle, and rode the 20 miles on her bicycle, and then in Les Baux (1917–21), Gignac, and Saint-Rémy in 1924.

In the meantime, she married Charles Mauron, a childhood friend of hers and of her family. Charles was only three years younger and was then a student in science at the University of Marseilles. Unfortunately Charles suffered from a retina problem and lost the vision in one eye,

Marie Mauron 1896–1986 (Photograph Editions Denoël, Paris).

which put an end to a promising career as a scientist. On the initiative of an English friend of theirs, Roger Fry, whom they had met in Les Baux, Charles translated E.M. Forster's *A Passage to India* into French, and in the following years, Virginia Woolf's *Orlando*, Catherine Mansfield, and Lawrence of Arabia. Besides her work as a teacher, household chores and the care of Charles, Marie also assumed the responsibilities of secretary to the mayor, and helped type the translations (fifteen books altogether). In 1930, the Maurons bought and restored an old *mas* where they entertained their numerous friends including painters Yves Brayer, Balthus, Fry, Foster and Woolf. Fry encouraged Marie to write and was responsible for the publication of her first novel in England (*Mount Peacock*, 1934).

Her literary career actually began during World War II with the publication of *Le Quartier Mortisson* (1941). The Maurons participated in the resistance and continued to write but Charles's health problems grew worse. In 1939, he went to Switzerland for another eye operation but without much success. Encouraged by the success of her book, Marie took early retirement from her job and devoted her time to liter-

ature. After the war, Charles and she separated and Marie lived in Saint-Rémy with her parents. She devoted her life to Provence and especially loved the Alpilles region dear to Mistral. Her early novels were largely autobiographical and retrace the life she had known as a young girl. In *Le Sel et les Pierres* (1942), Mauron tells the story of a twenty-two-year-old woman, Angélique Albran, who after her father's death, decides to leave the city and go back to the small village of Baumes-Rousses where she grew up. Angélique is a strong-minded woman, as are all of Mauron's female protagonists, and she wants her independence from men. Her return to the village is not without problems as the once thriving economy based on the quarry is now almost abandoned. Only a handful of people remain including Arnavelle, her father's wet-nurse, and Esprit, the café owner and occasional poacher. Even Trébizonde, her large family house, is in ruins. But Angélique is proud to be an Albran and determined to live on the land of her ancestors. With the help of Esprit and Pierre, a young poacher, she prunes the olive and almond orchards and cleans up the vineyards. After hard work and dedication, she becomes an inspiration to the remaining population. Angélique also renews contact with the people of her childhood such as the shepherds and gypsies.

Mauron wrote in French but her characters are supposed to express themselves in Provençal. The subject matter of her stories, the return to a traditional rural Provence, shows the impact of Bosco and Giono. However, unlike in the novels of her male predecessors, Mauron's female protagonists are vigorous women who seek their independence and do not restrain from doing a man's work. Mauron's style is uniformly simple and free of long descriptive passages either of nature or of her protagonists. Mauron had engaged on a literary career but she continued to take an active part in the defense of Provence. In 1946, she collaborated with Charles and Mr. Dourguin for *Lou Provençau à l'Escolo,* an association that sought to promote the teaching of Provençal in the schools.

Mauron's stories are always deeply rooted in the local traditions and customs. Her novel *Le Royaume Errant* (1953), for instance, is based on the tradition of *transhumance* or yearly sheep drive, and the world of shepherds. Following a fight with her husband Milien, Rosa and her daughter Nanon leave and go back to her town called Die in Higher Provence. Milien is happy to have gotten rid of them, enjoys being on his own and taking care of his farm by himself. One day he finds Constant the old shepherd, badly injured at the bottom of a small

ravine, and takes him to the hospital. To thank him for his help, and knowing that he does not have much longer to live, Constat gives Milien his flock of sheep. Milien then contacts Nègre, a shepherd from the Crau valley, and joins his family for the annual *amountagnage* or journey to higher grazing grounds. For three months Milien shares the lives of shepherds in the lower Vercors region and slowly learns how to care of sheep. In the meantime, he falls in love with Catherine, Nègre's daughter. On the way during a stop over in Die Milien visits his wife and obtains the custody of his daughter, Nanon. Catherine is ready to share Milien's life. The realism is poignant and Provençal countryside represented with precision and a gentle picturesque touch but particularly moving are the scenes in which Mauron describes childbirth, children and maternal love. Like in Daudet's novels, the tone is, on the whole, melancholy.

When she was not busy pouring forth novels, Mauron wrote about Provençal folklore and traditions. In the later part of her life she was also the recipient of many honors and awards (Palmes Académiques, Légion d'Honneur) and her books regularly received prizes (Prix George Sand, Mistral etc.). In a later novel called *Les Arsacs* (1972) Mauron tells the saga of a Provençal *mas* and its owners, the Arsacs, from the end of the nineteenth century to the 1970s with a particular emphasis on the radical transformation of rural life. Before the Great War the *mas* flourishes. The traditional crops of olives and almonds are complemented by a small silkworm farm and sufficient to feed Albin Arsac and his family. Life is hard but farmers are self-sufficient. Then, Albin loses his pregnant wife Annette who is killed by lightning. He raises his only son Regis with the help of his own mother. Then Regis is killed in the war in 1916. Albin hires a young housekeeper Nevia and ends up marrying her. A new family is born with three daughters. But Nevia is jealous of his former wife and does not like country life. When Albin dies she moves to town. World War II and competition in the modern world bring the *mas* to bankruptcy. Soon after the war Bernard, a sculptor, rents part of the mas. Nanon, one Nevia's daughters falls in love with him. The 1970s and the back to nature movement bring a little more hope to the farm and Bernard's sculptures, but only temporarily and the couple goes through the traditional problems. The dominant tone is, again, melancholy throughout.

On the contrary, humor characterizes *Il Pleut Il Fait Soleil...*(1975), a story reminiscent of Daudet. Nanie, Le Fena's daughter is pregnant

Pierre Magnan 1922 (Photograph Editions Denoël, Paris).

but her lover Tarcelin abandons her for another woman. Antonin, a transient worker recently hired by Fenant, loves Nanie and agrees to be a good father. Unhappy love and children born outside wedlock is also a theme dear to Pagnol. By her novels and books on local folklore Mauron contributed immensely to the popularity of Provence both in the capital and abroad. She died in her *mas* of Anginary in Saint-Rémy in 1986. She was ninety years old.

Among successful recent writers, Pierre Magnan certainly stands out as the most original and creative. Born in Manosque in 1922, *Lou picho Toinou,* (Small Tony) as he was then called after his father, grew up in a working class family in which the grandparents used mainly Provençal. His father was an electrician and a member of the newly created Communist Party and his grandfather a socialist. Magnan was an only child but was close to his older cousin Raymonde who would always hide his large ears in a beret. When his parents were away, Magnan loved to stay at his grandparents' where meals were eaten in absolute silence and where he would daydream for hours in the room above the stall. In his memoirs Magnan remembers vividly his father's bag or *biasso* which not only contained all sorts of tools but also brought back home the fragrances of the hills and particularly *pébre d'aï* (savory). As a child he would often visit his aunt Louise in her little grocery store

which smelled of herrings, cheese and spices, and his uncle Théophile who would give him slug juice to drink. He remembers Sundays at the silent movies and the cold schoolrooms only heated by a small wood stove and the strict discipline. Magnan says he learned how to read in the funnies *Les Pieds Nickelés* and the newspaper *Le Canard Enchaîné* that his father let him peruse before him every Wednesday evening and believes that his lack of curiosity about faraway places dates back from this time.[3]

Magnan was an adolescent when he met Giono. He was working as a printer's apprentice at the time. Like most people in Manosque, he knew who Giono was, and he and his friends would often catch a glimpse of the man with a large hat nonchalantly walking in the middle of the street or having a drink at the terrace of a café. With his light but striking blue eyes, pointy ears and long, fox-like nose Giono stuck out from the local population who still wondered how he was making a living since he had given up his position in the bank. Fifteen-year-old Magnan and his friend Jef wanted to create a magazine *Au-delà de la vie* and decided to ask Giono to write a preface. The two boys gathered up their courage, walked up to Giono's house and informed him of their project. Giono found the idea *épatante* and, stuffing his pipe invited the boys to join him and his group in the Contadour. Magnan was thrilled and from that day a long relationship, made up of friendship and reverence—Magnan always used *vous* with Giono—was born.[4] Magnan was, besides Giono, the only other *Bas-Alpin* or man from higher Provence at the Contadour in 1937. It was there on this high plateau, three thousand feet above Manosque, that Magnan, who up until that time had not read Giono, listened to him reciting excerpts from his upcoming book *Batailles dans la Montagne*. It was a revelation. For the first time he was presented with a book he wanted to read. It was not the love story that interested him but all the other characters who seemed so lively and real.

Magnan respected Giono and his ideal but it was the artist in him that fascinated him and especially the fluidity and limpidity of his prose and his new way of looking at things.[5] Every Sunday morning and sometimes also during the week after work, Magnan would walk up to Giono's house to borrow books: Tolstoy, Gogol, Claudel, but also Cervantes, Gide and Cendrars. Later Giono would lend him English and American novelists, but Magnan always showed a preference for French authors including Gide, Martin du Gard, Mon-

therlant and later Proust and Stendhal. Naturally his favorite author was Giono whose books he obtained through his friend Jacques Michel. Magnan enjoyed them all but particularly *Naissance de L'Odyssée* which he read over and over again. In 1939, Giono introduced Magnan to Mathilde Monnier, a fifty-three-year-old successful Marseillais author of popular fiction and soon a love relationship began. It lasted ten years. Magnan was her lover but also typed her manuscripts, helped her with her correspondence and took care of the house and dogs.

During the war, he was sent to the *Chantiers de Jeunesse,* a sort of work camp for French youth, and later he escaped deportation to Germany. Living surrounded by writers, it was only natural that Magnan followed in their footsteps. In 1940, Monnier's *Nans le Berger* was very well received by the press but Magnan always showed a marked preference for Giono, who listened to his stories and told him to work hard and to persist. Between 1938 and 1940, Magnan worked on a novel which was only published in 1993 entitled *Périple d'un Cachalot.* After the war Monnier contacted the publisher Julliard and helped Magnan publish his first novel *L'Aube Insolite* (1946) which was well received by critics but failed to interest the public as unfortunately did three subsequent novels. In 1949, and after his lack of success, Magnan left Manosque for twenty-seven years. He only saw Giono twice during that time. Magnan and his wife lived then in Nice where he worked for a refrigeration company until he was laid off in 1976.[6] He then seized the opportunity to resume his writing activity and this time achieved success.

Le Sang des Atrides (1977) takes place in Digne where, early one Monday morning, the garbage collectors find a man's body. Commissioner Laviolette, a fifty-two-year-old local man, is called to the scene of what the police suspect to be a crime, along with his friend judge Chabrand. Laviolette is a simple man who has had a few personal problems himself. His father has committed suicide and his own wife has left him for another man. He was drafted during World War II, fought bravely and received several medals. Laviolette has never remarried and at this time in life he is looking forward to retiring. The victim is soon identified as Jean Vial, a local bachelor. He has been killed by a blow to the temple caused by a blunt but heavy object and, at the time of the murder, was wearing cycling pants. Later the pathologist adds that the blow was caused by a large stone of the kind found on the banks of the River Bleone. During the following months, Lavi-

olette fails to find any new information and the case seems to be bogged down. But early in October, a strange accident occurs during a mountain car race. A young participant, Jules Payan, apparently loses control of his vehicle and falls into a ravine. Strangely enough there are no brake or skid marks on the road and the coroner's report indicates that Payan died of a lesion to the temple. Laviolette concludes that the young man must have been killed by a stone before losing control of his car.

Keeping the custom of most *Bas-Alpins,* the local people remain silent and both crimes seem to have been committed without witnesses. Digne is a friendly but secretive town and Laviolette begins to doubt if he will ever be able to find the murderer. However, several weeks after the second incident, two hunters pay Laviolette an impromptu visit and inform him of their strange discovery. While crossing the forest, they heard several thumps as though someone was hitting a target, and saw a shadow quickly disappear. The winter fog was thick and all the hunters could make out was something that looked like a short man with a beret and a cape. At the place where they heard the noise they picked up a road sign which had been used as a target and hit several times, probably by a stone picked up in the nearby river. Laviolette soon regains his confidence. The pathologist has just confirmed that, indeed, the second victim was killed by a stone, and adds that the fatal projectile must have been thrown with a powerful tool.

As winter sets in and snow falls, Laviolette begins to spy on the local population of his native town. He knows almost every one and is well respected but, except for the two hunters, no one seems to have noticed anything uncommon. A month goes by, and one night during their round in town, two policemen discover the lifeless body of Chérubin Hospitalier, a philosophy teacher. When found, he was lying on the floor near his bicycle and shows a similar head wound. However, this time there are more clues. First, before he died the victim had started to write down the letters *OR* in the snow, and, around a nearby statue, the killer had left a footprint. Laviolette is intrigued by the letters and sends a cast of the footprint to the lab. In a few days the lab reports that the shoe was made in the 1930s and that its owner is indeed short and lightweight.

The letters *OR* haunt him for days and do not seem to correspond to anyone in town but another clue comes from a television program on Brittany that Laviolette is watching and in which a young man demonstrates

the use of the traditional slingshot. Laviolette immediately calls Chabrand and tells him he knows what the murder weapon is. Unfortunately, in the meantime another person is killed. Once again, the murderer has used his slingshot but this time the victim is an older woman. Laviolette begins to suspect that love and Greek tragedy may be at the origin of the murders.

Magnan's book was well acclaimed. It was awarded the prestigious Prix du Quai des Orfèvres and sold over one hundred thousand copies. Commissioner Laviolette had managed to captivate the audience and Magnan emerged as a sort of Provençal Simenon. He did not waste time and immediately prepared another complex case for Laviolette. *Le Commissaire dans la Truffière* (1978) one of his best novels, which takes us to the small village of Banon, dear to Giono, on the high plateaus, near Manosque. The story begins with a scuffle between a brother and a sister arguing about family and inheritance. The young man is a hippie and informs his sister that he has wants no part of his father's factory and prefers to squander all of his inheritance money. Outraged, his sister knocks him on the head with a wrench and unintentionally kills him. His young dog escapes. As she is about to leave the forest where the scene takes place, a car pulls over. The woman hides in the bushes and observes the driver take a corpse from the trunk and disappear into a nearby cemetery. Unfortunately, on his way back to the car, the man notices the woman and attempts to kill her but she has the upper hand and with her gun forces the man to carry her brother's body into the same vault as his own victim, after which she escapes.

A few days later, Alyre Morelon and his truffle hunting sow Roseline wander about the countryside looking for truffles when Roseline is attracted by something she has noticed in the woods. She escapes Morelon's vigilance and when she comes back she is wounded. Morelon investigates the wood and finds a bucket with the residue of a liquid at the bottom and a hat with a net over it lying on the ground. The hat intrigues him for it is the kind used by beekeepers as well as the *Uillaoude* or local witchdoctor in order to ward off evil spirits. In the meantime, Laviolette arrives in that little village of nine hundred souls which has lately been the scene of several disappearances. During the last six months, five hippies, two women and three men, living outside the village in an abandoned church, have not given any sign of life and their worried parents have alarmed the police.

Laviolette takes up residence at the local hotel run by the friendly Rosemonde Burle, a warm, robust woman in her forties. It is now winter

and snow covers most of the ground. Laviolette contemplates the scenery with a frown, rolls himself a cigarette and decides to pay a visit to the Marquis of Bredes, a buddy of his from the resistance, who now lives in a family castle nearby. The two men talk about the good old times over a bottle of *Saint-Emilion* and Bredes mentions in passing that one of his books on witchcraft has disappeared from the library, probably stolen by a visitor during one of his soirees. The two friends also discuss the series of disappearances and Bredes agrees with Laviolette that the hippies must have been murdered.

His suspicions are confirmed the following Sunday, when the waitress of a Banon restaurant discovers a body in her walk-in freezer. The local *gendarmes* are called in and the pathologist's informs them that after being killed with a razor, the hippie had been entirely drained of his blood. The macabre news frightens the villagers and they finally begin to speak up. One of them tells Laviolette that recently he has seen an unusual car, a Renault 4 or a Volkswagen Bug driving around in the snow. Since the village was snowbound and all roads blocked off, Laviolette deduces that the murderer must live in the village and immediately starts looking for the mysterious car. Then, Arlyre informs Laviolette of Roseline's misadventure and of his discovery of a dog crying over a tomb in the cemetery. Laviolette calls in for more police help and then searches the cemetery. Soon the mysterious tomb reveals the missing bodies of the hippies, all but one, bled to death. It now seems clear that the killer is someone from Banon for he or she must have had a key to the cemetery. Laviolette believes that the key to the murders must lie in the stolen book on witchcraft and decides to pay another visit to his friend Bredes. Unfortunately when he arrives at the castle Bredes is lying on the floor with his throat slashed. Laviolette has seen a shadow disappear but remains near his dying friend. Bredes' maid informs him that she has seen a copy of the book in the attic. Laviolette gets hold of it, reads it and understands ... a very mysterious affair indeed. Magan's novel was another success but did not sell as well as *Le Sang des Atrides.*

Laviolette, like Magnan himself, is proud of being a *Bas-Alpin,* and his investigations reveal a Provence that is both secretive and violent. In Magnan's Provence, crimes are not committed haphazardly but as the result of long premeditation and in which traditions and family honor play an important role. Unlike Simenon, Magnan's plots are complex and deeply rooted in the past. The murderer is typically a serial killer whose personality eludes the most astute psychologist and whose crimes

are the results of extenuating circumstances. His next novel *Le Secret des Andrônes* (1980) takes place in Sisteron in the sixties. During a performance of *La Tour de Nesle,* Jeanne, Mrs. Rogeraine's nurse and also her niece, is thrown off the tower to her death. Fortunately a witness sees a mysterious person walking behind the victim dressed in a post office raincoat with a hood. Laviolette, present at the performance, picks up an interesting card lying a few feet away from the body with the name of Gilberte Valaury written on it. Rogeraine is a single woman in her fifties paralyzed from the waist down. She and her friends declare to Laviolette that they have never heard of Valaury and Rogeraine hires another nurse.

The plot thickens when, within a few days, the new nurse is also murdered in Rogeraine's own house, thrown, like the first one, from an attic window. Laviolette is not surprised to see the same card with the name Valaury pinned on the victim's body and suspects that Rogeraine and her friends are withholding information from him. He interviews them one after the other, Constance her maid, Rosa Chamboulive and her husband Vincent, Mr. Tournatoire the *notaire* and his wife Algae, Dr. Gagnon, the sisters Esther and Athalie Romance and cousin Evangeline who lives alone in nearby Ribiers, having recently buried her third husband. The murderer left no prints, and theft does not seem to be the motive, and the commissioner begins to think that the killer's intention was to isolate or scare Rogeraine. Vincent Chamboulive finally confesses that he knew Valaury and that she lived in a neighboring village, and, from Charlot the carpenter, he also learns that, shortly after the war, Rogeraine was shot by her husband when he surprised her with a lover. The latter then turned the gun on himself but she survived, paralyzed. Charlot shows Laviolette a photograph of Rogeraine and her two sisters with, in the background, a fourth young woman on a bicycle whose name he does not remember.

In the meantime Anna, a young hippie recently hired by Rogeraine, leaves Digne to hitch a ride toward Sisteron. Someone wearing a postman raincoat picks her up, offers her some hash, and, while she is high, takes her to an abandoned house and pushes her out of the attic widow to her death. Defenestration is an unusual method amongst killers and Laviolette suspects that the key to the murder lies in the past and searches for clues in the cemeteries. Eventually he discovers Valaury's grave next to an old house. Buried with her were her parents Antoine and Barbe. All died during World War II, on June 26, 1944. Laviolette searches the empty house and finds the body of the young hippie in the

backyard again with the same card: Valaury. Questioned with the photograph, Rogeraine faints and Tournatoire confesses that his father knew the Valaurys but that the only survivor is their son Pierre, now a monk in the Grande Chartreuse. Laviolette flies to Grenoble, meets Pierre who says that his family had been killed by French resistants over a quarrel and that his sister had been thrown out of the attic window before his very eyes. Rogeraine and her lover were among the resistants and Pierre was spared. But while Laviolette is in Grenoble questioning Pierre, Rogeraine and Dr. Gagnon her guest are found dead, poisoned by the wine they had consumed! The sequel is quite unexpected and the suspense lasts until the very end.

Unlike Giono, who only loved his high plateaus, Magnan feels at home in Manosque with a marked preference for the town he knew as a child when it was small and its inhabitants knew each other and spoke the same idiom. Laviolette does not like the modern constructions and regrets the loss of character and local accent. In *Le Tombeau d'Hélios* (1980) he investigates another uncanny series of murders. It all begins when Paterne Lafaurie, a farmer, dies while spreading pesticides on his trees. His family is suspicious and the autopsy reveals, indeed, that the chemical substance found in the victim's lungs is much stronger than a pesticide. The following day Félicien Dardoire, in charge of pest control in the region, informs Laviolette and Chabrand that several phials of poison used to kill badgers and foxes have been stolen from his car. Soon afterward Dardoire in his bathtub is bombarded from the window with these small containers and dies within seconds. Laviolette then learns that Dardoire's wife Elvire has recently committed suicide and that Lafaurie and Dardoire had formed an association with Severin Armoire, the *notaire*, Sidoine Hélios the scultpor, and Aubert de Chantesprit, owner of a hotel. Within the next days Armoire is killed as he puts on a pair of gloves, into which the little phials of poison have been placed and Chantesprit is murdered at home shaking the postman's gloved hand in which the phials are hidden. Death, once again, is instantaneous. Hélios becomes the prime suspect but shortly before he disappears in his turn, he informs Laviolette of his interesting love affairs between his models including Elvire.

Magnan's prose is rich and precise, and his characters speak the language they know. Sensuality and sex are often present in his novels and especially in *Les Charbonniers de la Mort* (1982). This time Magnan takes the readers to the Lure mountain, near Forcalquier, in 1910. There Brigadier Laviolette, our commissioner's grandfather, and his

friend *gendarme* Chabrand also related to the judge, face a very uncommon case. The first victims are a man and a woman who die while making love. According to Doctor Pardigon, who examines their bodies, they had absorbed, perhaps against their will, large doses of Cantharis, a potent aphrodisiac, and exhausted themselves in the act. Over the next weeks the same potion is responsible for the ecstatic death of several other couples, old and young. Only Bredannes the herborist knows the mysterious aphrodisiac formula but the killer secretly watches him. Unlike the preceding novels this one suffers from an overabundance of characters and romantic episodes. Magnan was perhaps getting tired of Laviolette and left him out of his following novel, *La Maison Assassinée* (1984).

The story takes place at the end of World War I. Séraphin Monge returns to civilian life and moves into La Burlière, an old house in higher Provence that he recently inherited, and gets a job as a road surveyor. Monge never knew his parents and was raised by the Sisters of Charity and then educated as a boarder at the College in Manosque. Old Burle, who works with him, knew his parents and explains to Monge for the first time the mystery of his past. When he was only three weeks old, his parents, two older brothers and grandfather were brutally murdered in La Burlière. He was found crying in his cradle. Some days afterwards three railway workers from Yugoslavia were found drunk, their boots covered with blood and although they always claimed their innocence, they were found guilty and executed in Digne. According to Burle, they were innocent, for theft was not the motive and the murder weapon was a *tranchet,* a cutting knife only used by locals. Monge is profoundly shaken.

During the following months he meets his new neighbors, and especially the young women such as Marie Dormeur, daughter of Célestat Dormeur the baker, and Rose, daughter of Didon Sépulchre the miller. Monge is a solid and handsome fellow and both Marie and Rose soon fall in love with him but, tormented by the murder of his parents, he refuses their advances. Haunted by the nightmares and visions of his dying mother, Monge begins to tear down La Burlière stone by stone. The event soon attracts many visitors including Patrice Dupin, a prosperous blacksmith from the village of Les Mées. Patrice is a war veteran who was badly wounded and his face is disfigured. One day, Monge is unexpectedly summoned to the nearby monastery of Ganagobie where a dying monk confesses to him that the night of the murder he was traveling by La Burlière and had taken shelter from the pouring rain under

a thick bush when he overheard the conversation of three men apparently ready to commit a crime. During the following weeks the monk was ill and confined to his bed. It was only later that he learned about the murders. Monge now becomes convinced that the death of his family has not been solved and that the killers are still at large. As he continues to demolish his house he finds a sugar tin hidden near the fireplace. Inside a large amount of gold coins glitter and three sheets of papers attesting that Célestat Dormeur, Gaspard Dupin and Didon Sépulchre had borrowed money (1200 francs or the price of approximately thirty acres of fertile land) from Félicien Monge, his father, at 23% interest. The total sum was to be reimbursed at the feast of Saint Michel in 1896, precisely the day before the murder. Monge begins to plan his revenge. The gold coins intrigued him for they were older than 1830, years before his own father was born.

Invited over to Patrice's house in Les Mées, Monge meets Patrice's mother and his widowed sister Charmaine who immediately falls in love with him. Upon his return home in Peyruis, he realizes that during his absence someone opened the sugar tin and looked at the papers without stealing anything. The following days the body of Gaspard Dupin is found at the bottom of his pond. He was apparently drunk when he slipped and drowned, but the police noticed that the edges of the pool had been made slippery with soap. Next, Charmaine is killed by Gaspard's ferocious dogs, mysteriously let loose and Didon Sépulchre is crushed by the grindstone of his mill. Then, one day, a stranger pays a visit to Monge and tells him that the night his family were killed he had come to the house for food and shelter and was in the cellar when the murder took place. He saw everything. Later Monge discovers a skeleton with two daggers one with the initial F M, his fathers' and another one with Z at the bottom of an abandoned well on his property. He immediately pays a visit to Zorme, a solitary man disliked by the community and his revelations are quiet unexpected...Masterly told, the story received the Prix RTL Grand Public. It was later translated in twelve languages and adapted to the screen.

Le Mystère Séraphin Monge (1990) is the sequel to Monge's strange destiny. Weary and distraught with his preceding adventures and what he has learned about his origins and family, Monge leaves town and travels east to the Queyras Mountains near Barcelonnette. There he finds a job as a woodcutter and spends his days felling trees for Mr. Polycarpe. The place is wild and dangerous, for, in the past; there have been several landslides. Recently a geologist has come to the village and asked

the few remaining peasants to leave their village because the soil, primarily made up of clay and shale, is unsafe and more mudslides are inevitable. But no one pays attention to the warnings. Monge rents a room from the local café owner Auphanie Brunel, a large matron who immediately falls in love with him. In the meantime, back in Manosque, Dormeur the miller is worried. The gold coins that Monge gave him haunt him and he wants to give them back and sends Tibère Saille, his apprentice, to look for Monge but when the latter reaches the village, Monge has not shown any signs of life for a few days...The plot of this novel sequel is not as well thought out or coherent as the first one and the usual suspense not always present.

In the interval between the first and the second Monge stories, Magnan returned to his old friend Laviolette who in *Les Courriers de la Mort* (1986) faces another series of inexplicable crimes. In the small village of Barles some 15 miles north of Digne, Emile Pencenat, a retired postman, spends his time digging his tomb in the old cemetery while his wife Prudence has an affair with Rose, the local female tobacconist. One day he finds an unstamped envelope lying on a tomb, addressed to a Miss Véronique Champourcieux in Digne and, being an honest citizen, Pencenat buys a stamp and mails it. A few days later, Miss Champourcieux is found dead in her apartment, stabbed with a rusty bayonet.

Laviolette now lives alone with his cats on his property of Popocatepetl, an unexpected inheritance. He retired five years ago and divides his time between rereading Proust and a good chat with old friends in the downtown cafés. It is Chabrand who over a bottle of *Sancerre* and a few roasted chestnuts solicits his help. Laviolette is indeed intrigued for Barles is his mother's village. The two men visit the victim's bourgeois apartment in town. Miss Champourcieux was a forty-three-year-old single woman, daughter of a rich industrialist, recently deceased, and apparently had no known enemies. There were signs of struggle though and she used an old gun against her assailant but it unfortunately misfired. Nothing appears to have been stolen but the killer did search the house. On the piano, Laviolette found the mysterious envelope and in it a letter with the following words: "comme vous mesurez il vous sera mesuré."

In the meantime, in Barles, Pencenat finds another envelope and again mails it. A few days later Ambroisine Larchet, a widow and Véronique's cousin is murdered while trying to hide a parcel in her well. The assassin approached from her behind and shut the heavy door of the well on her head, killing her instantly. In the house Chabrand and

Laviolette find the envelope and letter with the same sentence. They search Ambroisine's attic and amidst hundreds of souvenirs notice that a medium size box has been recently removed. The portrait of a very intriguing looking older man, and an almost complete collection of postal calendars 1870-1940 with the year 1912 oddly missing, attract Laviolette's attention. Judging by the footprints the killer was wearing old-fashioned studded shoes. Once more Laviolette suspects that the solution lies in the family and pays a visit to old Dr. Pardigon in a retirement home. Because of his profession, Pardigon knew just about everyone in Digne. And what Laviolette learns that day is, indeed, very interesting.

La Naine (1987) reads somewhat differently from Magnan's preceding stories. It is not quite a detective novel but crimes are committed. It takes place after World War I, as usual in higher Provence, where Nène, a female dwarf is in love with Jean, a fourteen-year-old boy. Nène is a full-fledged citizen and helps out the villagers with their chores, carries water and secret love messages, and according to popular superstition, many believe she can also cast spells because of her disability. Jean who works as a typographer and reads Balzac and Stendhal, refuses her advances because he is more interested in Germaine, a girl his own age. Unfortunately, one day, Germaine dies of typhoid fever. She had apparently drunk from La Calade, a fountain whose water was contaminated by sewage and had already caused several deaths. But Victor, Jean's arch enemy, informs him that he saw Nène give a bottle of the contaminated water to Germaine. Victor, also secretly in love with Germaine swears vengeance but someone kills him. In this novel Magnan successfully reproduces the warm and picturesque atmosphere of a small Provençal village in the 1920s: the quiet and slow pace of life and the joviality of its artisans and peasants but also their superstitions and untold secrets. Who could have guessed that the old man peacefully drinking his coffee at a shady café had, years ago, killed his wife by throwing her down the steep stairs and then buried her in a badger's hole? Even the mayor is not what he appears to be and rumors about his incestuous relationship with his sister have circulated for years.

Magnan's most recent novel *La Folie Forcalquier* (1995) takes us back to January 1871 in the village of Forcalquier, above Manosque. Bredannes, the grandfather of the Bredannes introduced in *Les Charbonniers de la Mort* is a thirty-five-year-old herborist and occasional bootlegger. While on his way home one night, he discovers the bodies of five men in a cave by the side of the road, two *gendarmes*, one

hangman and his assistants, their throats slashed. Theft does not seem to be the motive. The following day he learns that Zinzolin, a well-known highway bandit, has escaped and later, at a party given by Count Pons, Bredannes finds a letter on the floor with a cryptic message. At the same party the local priest, an odd character always ready to try Bredannes' new drinks and not always trustworthy with the villagers' confessions, is found dead lying slumped on the dining room table. A week later a peasant driven by remorse informs Bredannes that he and three other accomplices had been hired by a masked man to kill the *gendarmes* and the other men. Shortly after, Bredannes finds the body of the peasant in a bush and learns that his three henchmen have also met with accidental deaths! Furthermore, he is informed that Lulu, the street lamp lighter intimately familiar with everything that went on at night in the village, has fallen off his ladder under strange circumstances.

This time, Bredannes becomes enraged, for Lulu was a friend of his and he swears to find the mysterious masked man. Later, in the forest where he was looking for new plants, the herborist finds Zinzolin, wounded. Then the plot branches out into several different love stories. Bredannes is a sensual man who likes mature women, especially large-bosomed ones, married or unmarried, but he is loved by Aigremoine, Ponce's daughter who, for some mysterious reason wants to kill Zinzolin...A very complex plot where sex and family honor are again inextricably woven together. Magnan is perhaps one of the rare Provençal authors to have been successful in the detective genre and his stories not only show a great talent but have also the merit of revealing the generally ignored dark side of Provence. He lives with his wife in Revest-St-Martin, near Forcalquier.

Jean-Claude Izzo is another novelist who recently achieved success in the detective genre, but this time it is not higher Provence's secrets but Marseilles' mysterious underworld that is unveiled. Born in 1945 in Marseilles, the son of an Italian father and Spanish mother, Izzo worked as a journalist and then editor of *La Marseillaise* for nine years before turning to novel writing. Camus, but also Brauquier and Giono, especially in *Le Chant du Monde,* are among his favorite authors.[7] His stories take place in Marseilles of which he gives realistic portraits from the fifties to the present. Written in the local dialect, a mixture of French and Provençal, Izzo's novels describe the world of petty criminals, mafiosi, prostitutes, and drug dealers. In *Total Kheops* (1995) named after the title of a rap song, Izzo introduces the character of Fabio Montale, a police inspector born and raised in *Le Panier,* Marseilles' working

Jean-Claude Izzo 1945–2000 (Photograph Editions Gallimard, Paris).

class district, dear to Bosco and Pagnol. Montale investigates the murder of his childhood friend Ugo, who back in town to avenge the death of his buddy of Manu, shoots Zucca, a famous Mafioso. Soon after the murder Ugo is killed in his turn. In the meantime, Leila, the daughter of an Arab friend of Montale's, is found dead on a small country road near Aix where she was a student. She has been raped and shot twice. Montale is enraged for he once loved her and swears to avenge her death. But the case is more complicated than he thought.

In Izzo's next novel *Chourmo* (1996) Montale has given up his job with the police. He is disillusioned with the mission of the police and cannot stand their dangerous deals with the mob and local politicians. In fact, Montale is an idealist and a dreamer who likes blues, salsa, rock & roll and the poetry of Brauquier. He has never traveled much but enjoys fishing and, like Pagnol's Marius, loves the sea. Sentimentally he is a hopeless bachelor. He has had many affairs but all have failed, for he cannot commit himself. A chain-smoker, who enjoys a good bottle of wine or whiskey, Montale is reminiscent of Humphrey Bogart if it were not for his taste for local dishes, *bouillabaisse*, sardines *à l'escabèche* or *anchoïade*. One day his favorite female cousin Gelou comes to Marseilles from Gap and asks him for help. Her adolescent son Guittou has disappeared and she is very worried. Although he is no longer a cop, Montale rarely refuses to help people in trouble. He

contacts Serge, a homosexual social worker, but either gang members or the police kills the latter in front of him. Later, Montale learns that Guittou has been shot in a famous architect's home. The plot thickens when he learns that Gelou, whose husband was killed by the Mafia in his own restaurant, now lives with a famous crook and killer!

Neither Pagnol nor Bosco would recognize Montale's Marseilles. Those days are gone forever, and the harbor has lost its eminence and some of its pride. After the French colonies gained their independence and the unions became more powerful, the economy plummeted and a certain malaise set in. The once famous joviality of its inhabitants that Montale experienced as a child seems to have vanished. *Les Marins Perdus* (1997) largely written under the influence of the poetry of Brauquier describes the lives of the few remaining sailors of the *Aldébaran* abandoned to her fate in Marseilles by bankrupt owners. Most of the sailors have left except Abdul the Lebanese captain, Diamantis, a Greek and Nedim, a young Turk. The story begins when young Nedim, before leaving for home in Istanbul, meets two women in a bar. Gabby and Lalla get him drunk until he is broke and he finally gets thrown out of the place by the bartender who keeps his passport and gear as collateral until he comes back to pay for the champagne. Nedim swallows his pride and tells his unfortunate story to Diamantis who, a few days later, goes to the bar to get Nedim's passport back. Gabby is actually Diamantis's former lover and the two unexpectedly meet again. She now lives with Ricardo, a local gangster. The plot thickens when Diamantis learns that Lalla is in fact his daughter. Shortly after the astounding news Diamantis is mugged by two men...Izzo died of cancer in January 2000.

Recently several Marseillais authors have written in the detective genre using their vernacular, a mixture of French and words of Provençal origin. Some of them have even provided a small lexicon at the end to explain the terms to non-Provençals. Stories such as *Trois Jours d'Engatse* (1994) by Philippe Carrese met with unprecedented success. It tells the incredible adventure of Bernard Rossi a stone mason who after an old neighbor of his is shamelessly run over by a police officer decides to avenge her death. Realistic language and picturesque bar scenes alternate with a nightmarish succession of violent murders, but humor is never absent and the result is a very entertaining book that has had the Marseillais public running to the bookstore since its publication. Michèle Courbou's *Les Chapacans* (1994) and René Merle's *Treize reste raide* (1997) are other examples of detective novels written in the dialect

and taking place in Marseilles that also met with unexpected success among the local population. For all these writers, Izzo included, the choice of Marseilles is not due to the city's reputation for crime, always exaggerated by the media which make it look like a good place for a detective novel or film. It is simply because it is a city they love and are proud of. However, the use of Marseillais idiom in this genre is a novelty and a new venture (one unforseen by the *Félibres*) that shows that for the first time ever the local language, and not just a few words or expressions added as a touch of local color as it traditionally was, finally found its way into literature. For the first time since World War II the future of Provençal culture no longer seems bleak. When Provençal becomes extinct as a literary mode, local idiom will probably take over.

As the present work has hopefully shown, Provence has had a long literary tradition, one which either preceded and eclipsed the French such as with the medieval troubadours or ran parallel to it following the Inquisition against Cathars. Expressing themselves in Provençal or in French, the writers of Provence chose to represent their attachment to their land and culture, striving, each in turn, to remain as genuine and authentic as possible. The Provence their works reveal is far from the one generally known through the usual clichés. The *Félibres* are the proud descendants of the medieval troubadours. Daudet's *Lettres de mon Moulin* contain some of the most poetic passages devoted to Provence although the protagonists of his novels tend to represent the Dionysian and comic aspects of Provençal men. Bosco attempted to communicate the evanescent and subtler aspects of Provence, glimpses of which he detected in the magic of Lubéron and the silent marshes of Camargue. Through myths and spirits his novels link us to the Roman and Greek past, a tragic past which also haunted Pagnol and lurks behind the poetry of Brauquier and the detective novels of Izzo. Giono fills the gap and brought higher Provence, long ignored, into the literary scene: forlorn plateaus and their handful of inhabitants last descendants of a vanished race. Magnan observes the apparently quiet provincial towns with the scrutiny of a commissioner to bring to light the most sordid stories.

Endnotes

1. "*Marius,* c'est *Et l'au-delà de Suez*, je te dois trois millions." Louis Brauquier, *Je Connais des Iles Lointaines: Poésies Complètes* (Paris: Table Ronde, 1994) 21.

2. "Mon culte pour Mistral et mon zèle félibréen enthousiaste, joints à mon nom de Roumanille ne me valurent pas des félicitations…. Je passai le cap de justesse." Marie Mauron, *Les Caprices du Destin* (Paris: Plon, 1981) 79. Cited by Michèle Rouchi, *Marie Mauron: Sa vie, son oeuvre* (Paris: Barré & Dayez, 1987) 45, note 1.

3. "J'étais déjà atteint d'une incuriosité totale pour les autres parties du monde." Pierre Magnan, *L'Amant du Poivre d'Ane* (Paris: Denoel, 1988) 278.

4. "J'étais au comble du bonheur. Moi dont la machine à me souvenir est si exacte d'ordinaire, ici je ne me souviens plus de la couleur, de la texture qu'annonçait le couchant ce soir-là. Giono m'avait éffacé le ciel." Magnan, *Pour Saluer Giono* (Paris: Denoel, 1990) 30.

5. "C'étaient les voix des lacs et des montagnes et le souffle des vents le juste mouvement de la vie irrésistible des personnages dressés devant le destin, puis abattus, puis ressuscités…c'étaient les dévastatrices stridences des trompettes de la mort qui retentissaient en lui, en un mot, ce que j'aimais en Giono, c'était ce tabernacle qui contenait la création." Magnan, 74.

6. Actually, he was transferred to Paris but his wife refused to go there, so he opted for unemployment. Interview with the author in Forcalquier on December 22, 1997.

7. Interview with author, January 15, 1998.

Works Cited

Ambart, Jean. *La Comédie en Provence au XVIIIe siècle*. Aix-en- Provence: La Pensée Universitaire, 1956.

Arène, Paul. *Jean des Figues*. Raphèl-les-Arles: Marcel Petit, 1979.

Audouard, Yvan. *Ma Provence.* Paris: Plon, 1993.

Baratier, Edouard, ed. *Histoire de Marseille*. Toulouse: Privat, 1987.

Bens, Jacques. *Marcel Pagnol*. Paris: Seuil, 1994.

Blanchet, Philippe. *Dictionnaire du Français régional de Provence*. Paris: Bonneton, 1991.

Bogin, Meg. *The Women Troubadours*. London: Paddington Press, 1976.

Bornecque, Jacques-Henry. *Les Années d'Apprentissage d'Alphonse Daudet*. Paris: Nizet, 1951.

_____. *Histoire d'une Amitié: Correspondance Inédite entre Alphonse Daudet et Frédéric Mistral 1860 1897*. Paris: Julliard, 1979.

Bosco, Henri. *Antonin*. Paris: Gallimard, 1980.

_____. *Les Balesta*. Paris: Gallimard, 1956.

_____. *Cahiers Henri Bosco 35/36*. La Calade: Edisud, 1995.

_____. *Le Chemin de Monclar.* Paris: Gallimard, 1962.

153

_____. *L'Epervier*. Paris: Gallimard, 1963.

_____. *L'Habitant de Sivergues*. Paris: Gallimard, 1935.

_____. *Hyacinthe*. Paris: Gallimard, 1940.

_____. *Un Oubli Moins Profond*. Paris: Gallimard, 1961.

_____. "Un Poète de la lune et des astres." *Le Figaro Littéraire*. October 19–25 (1970):14.

_____. *Le Récif*. Paris: Gallimard, 1971.

_____. "Mistral" in *Tableau de la Littérature Française: de Mme de Staël à Rimbaud*. Paris: Gallimard, 1974.

Boutière, Jean, and Schutz, A.H. *Biographies des Troubadours: Textes Provençaux des XIIIe et XIVe siècles*. Paris: Nizet, 1964.

Brauquier, Louis. "Bosco le Silencieux," *Les Nouvelles Littéraires*. November 14 (1968):6.

_____. *Je Connais des Iles Lointaines: Poésies Complètes*. Paris: Table Ronde, 1994.

Brun, Auguste. *Poètes Provençaux du XVIe siècle*. Gap: Ophrys, 1954.

Bruno, Lucien. *Manosque au Temps Jadis*. Manosque: Rico, 1975.

Caldicott, C.E.J. *Marcel Pagnol*. Boston: Twayne Publishers, 1977.

Calmels, Norbert. *Rencontres avec Marcel Pagnol*. Monaco: Pastorelly, 1978.

Carrière, Jean. *Jean Giono: Une Biographie et des Entretiens*. Besançon: Editions de la Manufacture, 1991.

Castans, Raymond. *Marcel Pagnol m'a raconté*. Paris: Table Ronde, 1975.

_____. *Marcel Pagnol: Biographie*. Paris: Lattès, 1987.

Cauvin, Jean-Pierre. *Henri Bosco et la Poétique du Sacré*. Paris: Klincksieck, 1974.

Chevaly, Maurice. *Giono à Manosque*. Saint-Maximin: Le Temps Parralèle, 1986.

Citron, Pierre. *Correspondance Jean Giono-Lucien Jacques*. Paris: Gallimard, 1981.

_____. *Giono*. Paris: Seuil, 1990.

Cleber, Jean-Paul. *Les Daudet*. Paris: Presses de la Renaissance, 1988.

_____. *La Provence de Pagnol*. Aix-en-Provence: Edisud, 1986.

Conrad, Joseph. *Notes on Life and Letters*. New York: Freeport, 1972.

Daudet, Alphonse. *Lettres de mon Moulin*. Paris: Presses Pocket, 1990.

_____. *Le Petit Chose*. Paris: Livre de Poche, 1984.

_____. *Numa Roumestan*. Paris: Librairie de France, 1929.

Dauphin, Léopold. *Paul Arène*. Béziers: Société de Musicologie du Languedoc, 1912.

Dumas, René. *Les Années de Formation de Joseph Roumanille*. Paris: Sorbonne, 1970.

Edel, Léon. *Henry James: A Life*. New York: Harper & Row, 1985.

Flaubert, Gustave. *Correspondance*. Vol. 3. Paris: Librairie de France, 1929.

_____. *Gustave Flaubert–George Sand: Correspondance*. Paris: Flammarion, 1981.

Gaillard, Lucien. *Victor Gélu: Poète du Peuple marseillais*. Marseilles: Laffitte, 1985.

Gardy, Philippe. *Un Conteur Provençal au XVIIIe siècle: Jean de Cabanes*. Aix-en-Provence: Edisud, 1982.

Gérard, Alain. *Le Midi de Daudet.* Aix-en-Provence: Edisud, 1988.

Gerstmann, Adolf. *Alphonse Daudet, sein Leben und seine Werke bis zum Jahre 1883.* Berlin: Auerbach, 1883.

Giono, Jean. *La Chasse au Bonheur.* Paris: Gallimard, 1928.

———. *Colline.* Paris: Grasset, 1929.

———. *De Homère à Machiavel, Cahiers Giono.* Paris: Gallimard, 1986.

———. *Journal.* Paris: Gallimard, 1995.

———. *Poids du Ciel.* Paris: Gallimard, 1989.

———. *Pour Saluer Melville.* Paris: Gallimard, 1974.

———. *Recherche de la Pureté.* Paris: Gallimard, 1989.

———. *Refus d'Obéissance.* Paris: Gallimard, 1989.

———. *Solitude de la Pitié.* Paris: Gallimard, 1932.

———. *Triomphe de la Vie.* Paris: Grasset, 1982.

———. *Voyage en Italie.* Paris: Gallimard, 1954.

———. *Les Vraies Richesses.* Paris: Grasset, 1937.

Girault, Claude. ed. *Henri Bosco: Lettres à Noël Vesper.* Lourmarin, 1986.

Godin, Jean. *Le Sens du Mystère dans l'Oeuvre de Henri Bosco.* Montréal: Presses de l'Université. 1966.

Goldin, Frederick trans. *Lyrics of the Troubadours and Trouvères.* New York: Anchor Press, 1973.

Goncourt, Edmond and Jules. *Journal,* vol. 2. Paris: Laffont, 1989.

James, Henry. *Partial Portraits.* London: Macmillan, 1888.

Jouveau, Marie-Thérèse. *Alphonse Daudet, Maître des Tendresses.* Aix-en-Provence: Jouveau, 1990.

Jouveau, René. *Histoire du Félibirige.* Aix-en-Provence: Jouveau, 1984.

Le Clézio, Jean-Marie. "Hommage à Jean Giono," *Le Figaro Littéraire.* October 19–25 (1970):14.

Legré, Marie Dumon and Pierre. *Un Humaniste du XIXe siècle: Ludovic Legré.* Marseilles: Laffitte, 1982.

Lubin, Georges, ed. *Correspondance de George Sand.* Vol. 15. Paris: Garnier, 1972.

Magnan, Pierre. *L'Amant du Poivre d'Ane.* Paris: Denoël, 1988.

———. *Pour Saluer Giono.* Paris: Denoël, 1990.

Maurel, Martin. *La Vielle et l'Epée: Troubadours et Politique en Provence au XIIIe siècle.* Paris: Aubier Montaigne, 1989.

Mauron, Claude. *Frédéric Mistral.* Paris: Fayard, 1993.

Mérimée, Prosper. *Correspondance Générale,* vol. 1. Paris: Le Divan, 1941.

Mistral, Frédéric. *Memori e Raconte.* Raphèle-les-Arles: Marcel Petit, 1980.

———. *Calendau: Pouèmo nouvèu.* Avignon: Roumanille, 1867.

———. *Lou Pouèmo dou Rose.* Paris: Lemerre, 1897.

Moucadel, Henri. *Maillane: Le Temps Retrouvé.* Marguerittes: Equinoxes, 1992.

Pagnol, Marcel. *Album Pagnol.* Paris: de Fallois, 1993.

———. *Cinématurgie de Paris.* Monaco: Pastorelly, 1980.

———. *Confidences.* Paris: de Fallois, 1990.

———. *La Gloire de mon Père.* Paris: de Fallois, 1988.

Ripert, Emile. *La Renaissance Provençale: 1800–1860.* Marseilles: Laffitte, 1978.

Roche, Alphonse. *Alphonse Daudet.* Boston: Twayne Publishers, 1976.

Rostaing, Charles. *Mistral: l'Homme révélé par ses Oeuvres.* Marseilles: Laffitte, 1987.

Rouchi, Michèle. *Marie Mauron: Sa vie, son oeuvre.* Paris: Barré & Dayez, 1987.

Rouré, Jacques. *Alphonse Daudet.* Paris: Julliard, 1982.

Sachs, Murray. *The Career of Alphonse Daudet: A Critical Study.* Cambridge: Harvard U P, 1965.

Suarès, André. *Marsiho.* Paris: Grasset, 1933.

Sussex, R.T. *Henri Bosco, poet-novelist.* Christchurch: University of Canterbury, 1966.

Werf, Hendrik van der. *The Chansons of the Troubadours and Trouvères.* Utrecht: Oosthoek's Uitgeversmaatschappig, 1972.

Ytier, Robert. *Henri Bosco ou l'Amour de la Vie.* Lyons: Aubanel, 1996.

Zola, Emile. *Correspondance.* Vol. 2. Montréal: Presses de l'Université, 1980.

Index

DATE DUE

HIGHSMITH #45230

Printed
in USA